BIBLE CHARACTERS AND DOCTRINES

Mary, Mother of Christ to
The Gadarenes
E. M. BLAIKLOCK, M.A., D.Litt.

The Work of Christ
R. A. FINLAYSON, M.A.

William B. Eerdmans Publishing Company
Grand Rapids, Michigan

©1973 Scripture Union
First Published 1973
First United States Edition January 1974

Printed in the United States of America

Library of Congress Cataloging in Publication Data
Main entry under title:

Bible characters and doctrines.

   CONTENTS:
v. 3. Blaiklock, E. M. Nadab to Boaz. Wright, J. S.
The character of God.—v. 4. Blaiklock, E. M.
Elkanah to David. Grogan, G. The Holy Trinity.
               v. 7. Blaiklock, E. M.
Uzziah to Daniel. Ellison, H. L. The life of Christ.
[etc.]
   1. Bible—Study—Text-books. I. Blaiklock, E. M.
II. Wright, John Stafford. III. Grogan, Geoffrey.
BS605.2.B47   220'.07   72-189855

SCRIPTURE UNION IN NORTH AMERICA
U.S.A.:   1716 Spruce Street
          Philadelphia, Pa. 19103
Canada: 5 Rowanwood Avenue, Toronto 5,
          Ontario

INTRODUCTION

Each volume of Bible Characters and Doctrines is divided into the right number of sections to make daily use possible, though dates are not attached to the sections because of the books' continuing use as a complete set of character studies and doctrinal expositions. The study for each day is clearly numbered and the Bible passage to be read is placed alongside it.

Sections presenting the characters and doctrines alternate throughout each book, providing balance and variety in the selected subjects. At the end of each section there is a selection of questions and themes for further study related to the material covered in the preceding readings.

Each volume will provide material for one quarter's use, with between 91 and 96 sections. Where it is suggested that two sections should be read together in order to fit the three-month period, they are marked with an asterisk.

The scheme will be completed in four years. Professor E. M. Blaiklock, who writes all the character studies, will work progressively through the Old and New Testament records. Writers of the doctrinal sections contribute to a pattern of studies drawn up by the Rev. Geoffrey Grogan, Principal of the Bible Training Institute, Glasgow, in his capacity as Co-ordinating Editor. A chart overleaf indicates how the doctrinal sections are planned.

In this series biblical quotations are normally taken from the RSV unless otherwise identified. Occasionally Professor Blaiklock provides his own translation of the biblical text.

DOCTRINAL STUDY SCHEME

	Year 1	Year 2	Year 3	Year 4
First Quarter	The God who Speaks	Man and Sin	The Work of Christ	The Kingdom and the Church
Second Quarter	God in His World	Law and Grace	Righteousness in Christ	The Mission of the Church
Third Quarter	The Character of God	The Life of Christ	Life in Christ	The Church's Ministry and Ordinances
Fourth Quarter	The Holy Trinity	The Person of Christ	The Holy Spirit	The Last Things

DOCTRINAL STUDIES
THE WORK OF CHRIST

Study

Sacrifice in the Old Testament

Redemption in the Old Testament

Suffering in the Old Testament

The Teaching of Jesus

Study

CHARACTER STUDIES

MARY, MOTHER OF CHRIST
TO
THE GADARENES

Study

THE WORK OF CHRIST

Introduction

While it is all-important to know what Christ understood to be His own mission in the world and what it was to accomplish, it is not all we have to guide us. It is clear that much of His understanding of His mission and of the experiences through which He passed was mediated to Him through the Old Testament Scriptures, through ritual and sacrifice, through psalms and prophecy. It is equally clear that it required the testimony of His apostles, whom He had specially appointed to maintain and apply His witness (Acts 1.8), to give their interpretation of His mission, and that for this task He promised them the help of His Holy Spirit (John 16.12 f.). Thus it is that the Old Testament Scriptures, the Gospel records, and the apostolic writings from Acts to Revelation are our sources, and contain all we know and need to know of the mission and work of the historical Christ.

THE WORK OF CHRIST

Sacrifice in the Old Testament

It is evident that there had been a primitive revelation given
to a man of which Gen. 3.15 is a summary; moral evil would
eventually be destroyed (its head bruised), but at the cost of
suffering (the heel bruised). It may be assumed that when
God, in figurative language, gave this revelation to primitive
man, He also indicated the symbolic rite by which it would
find expression until the hour of divine action had struck.
The sacrificial shedding of blood not only kept this hope alive
through all the dark ages of the world's sin; it also shed
light on the way it could be accomplished. Faith grasped at
this, and through sacrifice maintained its contact with the
promise and its eventual fulfilment. Modern man often finds
the idea of blood-sacrifice difficult or even revolting. The
sacrifices showed clearly, however, that the God who
graciously provided a way for men to be reconciled to Him
also hated the sin that had caused the separation between
them. Further, such sacrifices made men treat the fact of sin
seriously.

1 : Abel's Sacrifice

Genesis 4.1–16

The distinction between Abel's form of sacrifice and Cain's
is at first sight difficult to determine, since they both offered
to God the fruit of their work. Abel, the shepherd, offered a
lamb from his flock; Cain, the agriculturalist, offered the
produce of his fields. Yet to Abel's offering God 'had regard'
and to Cain's He did not (4 f.).

It is significant that the offering was seen through the
medium of the offerer's character. And so it is emphasized
that God had regard to Abel *and* his offering, but to Cain and
his offering He had not regard. In each case character was
the determining factor.

Furthermore, the character was reflected in the nature of
the offering. A sacrifice has been defined as 'that outward

thing which best expresses one's feelings towards God and through which we offer ourselves to God' (Marcus Dods). Their respective offerings, then, were a decisive clue to the spirit of the two brothers. If the lamb slain best expressed Abel's feelings towards God, then he must have felt that he had amends to make to God, and that a life must be given for a life.

While we cannot elaborate a doctrine of atonement from this one passage, it is suggestive of a state of spirituality on the part of Abel that was truly remarkable for so early an age. It is untenable except on the assumption of a primitive divine revelation. Put in New Testament terms, it expresses symbolically the wages of sin. It recognizes that death is the way by which sin is removed, defining thus a situation which ultimately called for the supreme sacrifice of God's Son.

Meditation : Am I a Cain or an Abel ?

2 : The Sacrifice of Isaac

Genesis 22

The 'testing' of Abraham was a testing of his faith to strengthen and deepen it, and so enrich his character that he might be a guiding light to future generations. At God's command he was to offer his son Isaac to Him on Mount Moriah. That is the plain biblical statement of the case. Though human sacrifice was practised by the heathen peoples around, we are not left to assume that Abraham mistook the tangled confusion of superstition and ignorance belonging to primitive pagan faith as the voice of his God. As the proceedings develop we are not at all sure but that it was Abraham himself who was being placed on the altar!

In the whole of the Old Testament there is no sterner test of faith than this, and when he emerged triumphant, he was entitled to the honoured name: 'The father of all who believe' (Rom. 4.11). The elements in the testing are delicately brought out in the narrative.

It was a test of natural affection (note the phrasing of v. 2); it was a test of faith in God, since Isaac was 'the child of promise' through whom all the promises of blessing given to Abraham were to be fulfilled; it was a test of obedience, and on that one command Abraham set out immediately on a

13

three days' journey (3), each mile of the road presenting its own challenge, till at last Abraham felt he must complete the journey with Isaac alone (6). There was only one secret he could not yet share with Isaac, not even in answer to the question: 'Where is the lamb for a burnt offering?'. He pointed to God as the only answer he could provide (8). In short, it was a faith that was not based on understanding; it defied all the appearances of the situation, believing that somehow or other God would fulfil His promise to bless the world through that very Isaac he was to lay on the altar, even if it meant raising him from the dead (5, cf. Heb. **11**.19).

While the incident makes clear that the God of Abraham, unlike the gods of the neighbouring tribes, did not demand human blood as the sacrifice of faith, it lays bare the principles on which God's own faithful love worked and sacrificed for the salvation of the world (John **3**.16). In depth of feeling on the part of Abraham, and of obedience on the part of Isaac, it finds its counterpart and real fulfilment only in the journey of Jesus Christ from Galilee to Jerusalem to lay Himself on the altar of sacrifice for the world's sin. And God 'did not spare his own Son' (Rom. **8**.32).

Christ adds the footnote to Abraham's life: 'He rejoiced that he was to see my day; he saw it and was glad' (John **8**.56). If there is one place where the vision broke in on Abraham's faith, it was surely on Mount Moriah in the provision of a substitute for Isaac.

3 : The Passover Lamb

Exodus 12

Someone has compared the Old Testament to a room richly furnished but dimly lighted. The introduction of a light does not add anything to what is there, but it shows it more clearly. It is the light of the New Testament that adequately illumines this chapter. Here the Old Testament begins to be charged with the gospel that reached its climax in Christ. The rite of the Passover is our first example of the blood of sacrifice not only shed but applied to secure deliverance from slavery and servitude, and provide the security for joyful fellowship and communion. The application of the blood was faith's obedient acceptance of what God provided.

Danger threatened the families of Israel in Egypt as it did

all the families of the land. The angel of retribution demanded the life of the first-born of every family; the first-born being representative of the whole family which in its entirety was subject to death. From this the families of Israel were exempt only in compliance with a divinely ordered provision to which obedience would have to be given in every detail. Historically it signalled the immediate departure of Israel from the bondage of four hundred years in Egypt, and without doubt there is a parallel between the historical Exodus and the Messianic deliverance consummated in the death of Christ.

A lamb without blemish, taken from the flock, kept under scrutiny for four days, then killed (though not a bone of its body was to be broken), and its blood sprinkled on the outer doors of the Israelite homes, while its flesh was roasted to provide a banquet for the family within: these are the details. The only explanatory note provided with regard to the ritual was that the sight of the blood sprinkled on the outer doors directed the angel of destruction to pass over: hence the name Passover, by which the festival has been known ever since. In the morning the exodus from Egypt began.

This ritual that marked the birth-pangs of the nation of Israel had been observed throughout the years until Christ came. It was He who turned the Passover into the Lord's Supper (cf. Luke 22.19 f.) when at a certain stage He put aside the Pascal lamb—called 'the body' by the Jews—and, so to speak, placed Himself on the table, saying: 'This is my body.' The ancient ritual did not really save—no ritual does—it was merely a stay of execution until He should come who was Himself the First-born of the family of God (cf. Col. 1.15, 18). For Him, therefore, there was no 'passing over', since He was Himself the true Passover Lamb, the Lamb taken from the flock, without blemish, a bone of whose body was not broken in death (John 19.36).

As the stars of night fade into the light of day, so this expressive ritual of the Old Testament faith faded in the noon-light of Christ's sacrifice for the sins of the world (cf. 1 Cor. 5.7).

4 : Sacrifice and Restoration

Leviticus 1 (See also chs. 2–7)

The Book of Leviticus, i.e. of the Levites, established in

greater detail the implication of a sacrificial relationship to God. As Exodus emphasizes redemption (deliverance) by God, so Leviticus emphasizes the restoration of a redeemed people to communion with God. This restoration is secured by sacrifice.

The code of sacrifice as given to Moses was specific and detailed. The word 'sacrifice' here includes all gifts given to the Lord. The nature of the offerings is graded from the more to the less costly according to the circumstances of the offerer. Besides oxen, sheep and goats, fowls or doves were accepted from the very poor. An atoning function belonged, however, to all the offerings of whatever kind. In other words, they each provided ritual cleansing from sin. The principal applicable to all was that of completely voluntary offering (3).

The burnt offering is so named because it was laid on the altar and burnt in its entirety: hence *whole* burnt offering. It must be the offerer's own property, without blemish (on the principle of 'only the best for the Lord'). The offerer must lay his hands on the animal's head and confess his sins over it, so transferring his sins, figuratively, to the animal. The animal becomes a sin-bearer, and so it is slain by the offerer and burnt completely on the altar. The sprinkling of blood by the priest is evidence that life had been given. In its original institution it is therefore clear that the burnt offering was also a sin offering, though in its further implications it became a token of self-surrender and devotion to God, of which expiation (making satisfaction for sin) was an integral part (4).

Other offerings were introduced in particular cases. The sin offering (4.3) dealt with the sense of guilt and conveyed the assurance of pardon and restored fellowship. The guilt offering (5.6) dealt with a specific wrong done, rather than with sin in general, and sought forgiveness and restored peace. The peace offering (3.1) dealt with estrangement and sought access to God and fellowship. The cereal offering (2.1)—a bloodless offering—was an expression of gratitude to God and sought continuance in His favour. Note that in each case there was a symbolic identification of the offerer with the offering. The subjective elements represented penitence and joy.

The sacrifices, operating within the covenant God made with Israel, did not represent man's expedient for his own redemption. They were all forward-looking. The atonement

16

made was a 'covering' for sin until it should be put away by the sacrifice of Calvary. We shall see later how the New Testament makes this clear.

5 : The Two-Goats Sacrifice

Leviticus 16

The sacrifices detailed here all belong to the ritual of the Day of Atonement, the high festival of the Jews, the annual day of national penitence and cleansing and the removal of 'all the iniquities of the people of Israel' (21).

The significance for us here is that we are introduced to a new form of sacrifice, that comprising two animals. It required this compound sacrifice to express the complete putting away of sin. It is significant, too, that the one sacrifice comprised both death and life: one animal was killed, the other was led alive into the wilderness.

We are told (8) that one of the goats was 'for the Lord', and the other 'for Azazel' (NEB 'precipice'; AV 'scapegoat'). Azazel is merely a transliteration of the Hebrew word and may be a personalized name for a state of abandonment. It would appear that the two goats represented two aspects of man's sin; his guilt before God, and his personal defilement.

One goat was for 'a sin offering' (9). Though there is no specific reference to the laying on of the hands of the offerer, (see Isa. 53.6), it is emphasized that it was 'the goat of the sin offering which is for the people' (15). The animal is killed and its blood brought inside the veil and sprinkled on the mercy seat and before the mercy seat. This atoned for sin in its guilt.

Afterwards the other goat was brought to the High Priest and with the laying on of his hands he confessed 'all the iniquities of the people of Israel, and all their transgressions, all their sins' (21). The animal, now a sin-bearer, was not fit to be put back among the flock, but was led into the desert and there let loose, never to be seen again. It bore man's personal defilement.

It is noteworthy, therefore, that in this one offering for sin there were both atonement for sin and separation from sin: deliverance from its guilt in the sight of God, and from the blight of its curse in life and character.

17

The New Testament alone sheds light on this peculiar offering. It found its complete fulfilment in the sacrifice at Calvary. There were death and life in that sacrifice. On the cross Christ went alive through the experience that sin-bearing meant, and it was only when He cried 'It is finished' that 'he bowed his head and gave up his spirit' (John 19.30). In that ordeal which culminated in death He had entered a territory of suffering that the foot of man had never trod before, having been made a curse for us (Gal. 3.13). This received its outward expression in the historical fact that He suffered 'outside the gate' (Luke 23.33, cf. Heb. 13.12).

6 : The Abuse of Sacrifice

Jeremiah 7

Here we move from priest to prophet, from ritual and sacrifice to providential happening and ethical conduct (cf. Mic. 6.6 ff). This is Jeremiah's 'Temple Sermon' containing his denunciation of mere externalism in religion. To Judah 'the temple of the Lord' (note the repetition to signify reverence) was not only sacred, but the symbol of God's special care, of them. All who reverenced it were to be regarded as special objects of divine protection (4).

The prophet fearlessly exposed this fallacy. He charged them with oppression and idolatry, and with the hypocrisy of resorting to the Temple between acts of robbery and violence to receive the cover of its protection. This led him to speak of the Temple as 'a den of robbers' (11, cf. Matt. 21.13). To their violence and rapacity they added gross idolatry, burning incense to Baal (9), and 'making cakes for the queen of heaven' (18), a reference to the Babylonian worship of Ishtar, practised mainly by women. They even indulged in the hateful and inhuman practices of Moloch worship (31).

But while living lives of apostasy, dishonesty, and violence, they resorted to the outward ritual of temple worship, bringing their sacrifices to God as formerly. In the name of God, Jeremiah demands their abandonment of this mockery of religion (3–7). In v. 21 he gives them the counsel of contempt, advising them to add their burnt offerings (which were meant to be wholly burnt) to their other sacrifices and use them for food, since, for God, they no longer had the significance of sacrifice. In other words, the sacrifice had lost its entire spiritual value when offered in an unworthy spirit.

Jeremiah further reminds them that in the most illustrious era of their history, when God had intervened to bring them out of Egypt, the sacrifice of beasts was not required of them and so could not be the ground of their deliverance, although they were to sacrifice *after* their deliverance (see Exod. **5**.3; **10**.25). What God had required of them was obedience, to His will as the condition of His presence and intervention on their behalf (23). The Decalogue and not a sacrificial system, was the basis of the divine Covenant, requiring their obedience in character and conduct. This basic requirement the nation soon forgot, and the evil not only persisted but was aggravated in Jeremiah's day. Yet they continued to offer their sacrifices in the vain hope of averting the judgement of God on their corrupt lives.

This mere externalism in religion Jesus strongly condemned (Matt. **23**). Paul also dealt with this abuse (Gal. **5**.6). An unethical religion has no support from a gospel that is founded on the obedience and death of Christ. And this outlook is not yet dead.

Questions and themes for study and discussion on Studies 1–6
1. Why do you think there is so much slaughter of animal life involved in the sacrificial system of the Old Testament (cf. Heb. **9**.17–22; Lev. **17**.11)?
2. From your own reading of Abraham's life, in what circumstances do you think he 'saw' Christ's day (John **8**.56, cf. Gen. **15**; **22**.13 ff.)?
3. In what respect would you say the Passover, and indeed all the sacrifices, merely represented a stay of execution (cf. Rom. **3**.25)?
4. Does the assumption that Jeremiah as prophet is belittling the office of priest and the offering of sacrifice find support in his denunciation of unworthy sacrifice (Jer. **7**.22)? See his vision of the day when worship shall be purified and sacrifice shall fulfil God's intention (Jer. **17**.26).
5. With reference to externalism in religion, which Jeremiah denounces, do you think we have a present-day example in the tendency to make attendance at the Communion service the whole of religion (cf. 1 Cor. **11**.27–32)?

CHARACTER STUDIES

7 : Between the Testaments

Psalm 119.161–176; Hebrews 11.32–40

Four centuries lie between the ministry of Malachi and the birth of Jesus, the Messiah whose coming Malachi saw afar. Over those long momentous years history did not stand still. Brave men lived, trusted, died for their faith, and Israel regained her freedom only to lose it again. Alexander, at the head of a Greece which he had united by the sword, struck a death blow at the sprawling Persian Empire and broke it up. Alexander might have built a united world had he not died in Babylon, at the age of thirty-three, in the year 332 B.C.

His Empire fell into four parts, and Palestine was part of Syria, save when Egypt under its Greek kings of Alexandria, disputed the claim. As ever, Palestine lay, a buffer and a battleground, between the powers to the north and the power to the south. As Syria weakened, areas to the west, south, and east of her empire, which originally stretched from the Aegean to the Persian Gulf, and from the Caucasus to Sinai, asserted their independence, and the Jews had their century of freedom.

Some of the story of the years between the Testaments is found in the Apocrypha, often printed between the testaments of the NEB and RSV. Many of the great men and women of those days, though not 'characters of the Bible' in the strict sense of the word, are worth meeting—the family of the Maccabees, for example, Mattathias the dynamic and saintly priest who raised the Jewish standard of revolt against the tyranny of Syrian Antiochus; John, Simon, Judas, Eleazer and Jonathan, his sons, who bravely fought the battle through, amid toil, peril, tragedy and triumph; and the valiant Jews who fought beside them.

In other books of the Apocrypha we meet personalities who have had a place in Scripture. The Books of Esdras, for example, tell stories about characters of the Restoration. Susanna, and Bel and the Dragon, those ancestors of the detective story, reveal facets of Jewish life in which Daniel was a known and familiar figure. We meet again Baruch, the companion and secretary of Jeremiah, and we meet for the first time Joshua, the son of Sirach, who left a 'book of wisdom'. There are fictional characters like Judith, another Joel of the days of the Assyrian invasion, and the pious Tobit of the same period.

It is all fascinating reading, and helps the reader of the New Testament to understand what formed and shaped the character of the people whom he meets, restless under the domination of Rome in the time of Christ and the early Church.

8 : The Ancestors

Matthew 1.1–17; Luke 3.23–38; Numbers 27.1–11; 36.1–13

The prescribed readings may seem uninteresting. In fact, they are of some importance. The genealogies in the two Gospels will manifestly not be contradictory. They are as obviously different. Why? Numbers **27**.1–11 and **36**.1–13 are probably the key to the difficulty. Moses doubtless delivered thousands of judgements (Exod. **18**.12–27). Why among them all is this one mentioned? At first sight it merely determines that daughters who are heirs to their father's property shall marry within their tribe in order that the distribution of tribal possessions shall not be disturbed. But the law means more than this. It enabled the Lord as 'son of Mary' to be 'King of the Jews'. Mary, in order that her son (who would be legally considered Joseph's son) might inherit Judah's throne, had to marry within the tribe. It thus becomes of some importance to prove that Joseph was one of the tribe of Judah. This Matthew undertakes to do, quite in accordance with the preoccupation with kingship which characterizes his Gospel. In Luke, Joseph is called the 'son of Heli'. Heli must have been Mary's father, and Joseph is called his son because he was Mary's husband and his legal heir in the absence of any brothers of Mary. The word 'begat' or 'father of' is not used in Luke. Jesus on Mary's side sprang from Judah (Luke **3**.33) and His inheritance was effective because Mary married a true descendant of Judah.

Look closely at the lists. We have met many of these people before, observed their blemishes, their sins, their follies. Judah is in the list, David, Solomon, Rehoboam, even

Manasseh. Of such fallible human beings, after the flesh, came the Lord. God works out His purpose, as the whole of the Old Testament shows, by means of men and women, sometimes in spite of them, sometimes with their active co-operation, seldom with their complete and whole-hearted committal. It stirs our faith to know that so He worked through the long years of history during which He prepared the way for the coming of His Son. We shall see such divine working through the men and women of the New Testament . . . As we stumble on, and see around us, and indeed within us, failure, obtuseness, and lack of understanding, as we are confronted with disaffection, backsliding and apostasy, it is good to know that God's plan was always outworked amid the same frustrations. He will not fail today.

9 : Mary, Mother of Christ

Matthew 1.18–25; Luke 1.26–38; John 1.1–18

In the first chapter of the New Testament we meet the greatest woman of all time. Mary was no less. Reacting against attempts to bestow divinity upon her, Christians have too often denied Mary, the girl chosen to be the mother of Jesus, the honour which is due to her. She was a human being, and never more than a human being. So she appears in Scripture. She must, for all that, have been a woman of surpassing worth.

It was Mary's quiet habit to set deep in her heart the memory of momentous events in her experience (Luke 2.51), and to ponder on their significance. That was how it came about that, at the middle of the first century, when Luke, the physician, used the years when his friend Paul was in protective custody in Caesarea, to scour Palestine for facts (Luke 1.2 f.), he found Mary a mine of information.

He may, of course have met her in Ephesus, at the home of John, but meet her he certainly did, and the freshness of the Nativity stories in his Gospel must owe much to the vivid memory of Mary's old age. The Nativity probably took place about five years before the date calculated as late as A.D. 325, and still observed as the basis of the Christian calendar. Mary, therefore, was born somewhere before the year we call 20 B.C. Perhaps she was in her early seventies when she gave Luke the information which remained 'in her heart'.

She told him of the Annunciation, and the heavy burden of pain, misunderstanding and responsibility her girlhood was called upon to bear. The Virgin Birth, an essential teaching of Scripture, and vital for all respect for the authority of the New Testament, rests upon the word and testimony of Mary herself, and perhaps of Mary alone, for Joseph appears to have been long since dead. Those with sufficient hardihood of scepticism, may accuse the woman who has been honoured beyond all other women of falsehood, and the covering of girlhood fault or disaster by a specious tale, but Mary gives a notable impression of quiet goodness, of devotion to God, and utter purity. Luke, too, was no gullible simpleton, but a considerable historian in his own intellectual right.

Rather let us meet the Mother of Christ, a girl willingly given into God's hands, a woman of poetry and holiness, the human vehicle of God's greatest act in history.

10 : Mary the Psalmist

Luke 1.39–56; 1 Samuel 2.1–10

Tradition has it that Luke was an artist as well as a physician and a most notable historian. Certain it is that there is uncommon artistry in his writing. We are indebted to him for the preservation of the psalms of the early Church, which cluster in these chapters, and set the tone for Christian praise.

Mary's psalm, known from its first word in the Latin version as the Magnificat, reveals a facet of her choice character. It is a rewarding exercise to comb its ten verses through for Old Testament quotation and allusion, for it is laced with Hebrew poetry.

The poem throws light on the education of a Jewish girl, for Mary must have lived within the sound of Old Testament music, the words of ancient psalms and liturgy forming the pattern of her thought and self-expression. Observe that she had sought her cousin in her secluded dwelling in search of comfort and encouragement. Verse 39 follows significantly on its predecessor, as though to indicate that, as soon as the fulfilment of the Annunciation became conscious fact to her, Mary had sought the presence of one she had learned to trust for counsel and advice.

The task she had been called upon to perform was not

one which she bore placidly and without a natural surge of fear. She had no guarantee at all against hostile comment. It was altogether natural that she should need and seek the help of love and fellow-feeling. It was given her without hesitation, and in abundance. The result was an outpouring of song.

It is as though God requires some human nucleus on which to construct His blessing. Just as the tiny gift of loaves and fishes was multiplied to feed the throng by the lake, so, on the words of a loving and perceptive woman, He brought His surge of comfort and of fortitude to the Virgin's heart. And no blessing of God thus given can remain in fruitless storage. The gift of living water always becomes an upward-welling spring (John 4.14).

The three months' stay with the good Elizabeth is a silent period. Mary said nothing of the events or conversations of that time to the listening Luke. She must have needed solitude, limited fellowship and withdrawal. There are times when we all need them. Mary was preparing herself for great events. When great events come heralded and foreseen, the example of the wise young woman may well be followed.

11 : Joseph

John 6.22–59; Mark 6.1–6

Little is said of Joseph, the carpenter of Nazareth, save that he was a good man (Matt. 1.19). There could hardly be greater honour. Seeking to demean the Lord, those who thought much of status and position dismissed Him as 'the son of the carpenter', as though a father so inconsiderable brought little glory to his son.

But Joseph was an upright man, one of Israel's remnant. He moves humbly through a few brief pages of Scripture, overshadowed even by his noble wife. No word of ill is said of him. Almost equally with Mary, he was called to share the burden of the world's slander and gross misunderstanding. Called of God to do so, he carried the load without complaining. Given a command, he unquestioningly obeyed, and had the blessed task of protecting the Virgin and sheltering the Child.

There are multitudes of Christians like Joseph. They are

called to a simple task in an obscure environment. They hearken and obey. They do well and faithfully that which they are bidden to do: no one calls in praise; their thanks are the thanks that Joseph won, a loved one's smile, the love of a child. They are the salt of the earth.

Thousands of poems, hymns and carols cluster round Christmas. All the other characters of the story move in and out of verse and music. The shepherds crowd the inn. With the glitter of gifts the Wise Men come, adore, and go their way. Perhaps the place of Joseph in the story is emphasized in some poem, some forgotten fragment of verse. If that is so, long search this winter afternoon, at the world's end where this note on Joseph is written, has failed to find the reference.

Hence a touch of joy to write a word of praise for one who trod a hidden path, unseen, unregarded. He was merely the carpenter of Nazareth, whose good work and honest craftsmanship men took for granted, who took his fair and just reward for his careful work, spent it on his loved ones, and turned to the next day's task. The world would be a sweeter place were there more like Joseph. A good society is built of such good men, contented men who do the work they are fitted to do, men who house Christ in their homes, men who do their best, love their families, and leave no mark of evil on the world's marred face.

12 : The Innkeeper

2 Samuel 19.31–40; Jeremiah 41; Luke 2.1–7.

The innkeeper of Bethlehem has been misunderstood. He gave the weary family who had travelled down from Nazareth, the best he had to offer. Picture a square-cut cavern in the rock. At one end is a raised platform, where the ancient host quite naturally, and with never a thought of slighting them, disposed of his passing guests, in sight of their tethered beasts and stacked luggage. Bethlehem was full that night, for Bethlehem's absent population was home, at the command of totalitarian Rome, for the census. As a visitor of David's line, Mary might naturally have expected the best accommodation of the local hostelry. His 'kataluma' or guest room, which should not be translated 'inn', was already occupied. 'There was no room in the guest chamber.' Why?

Hillel, the great Pharisee, was of the royal line, like Mary, and would perhaps be there that day. He was over a hundred years old. His son, Simeon, would also be there. So perhaps would his grandson, Gamaliel, the teacher of Paul. Did this considerable party arrive first and fill the innkeeper's accommodation? The stable sleeping place was his second best. The manger was a cosy rock-cut recess.

Is it possible to say a little more? Jeremiah (**41**.17) speaks of a certain 'geruth', or 'inn', which is 'near Bethlehem'. It was in the possession of one Chimham. Was this a descendant of Chimham, son of Barzillai, who, because of his father's beneficence to the exiled David (2 Sam. **19**.31–38), was treated by the king as a son? Did he become thus, as the son of a great sheep-rancher, the steward of the royal sheep-lands at Bethlehem? Did he build a hostelry which remained in the family after the stable fashion of the East, to provide a refuge in Jeremiah's day, and a rendezvous for shepherds (Luke **2**.15) in New Testament times?

Was the innkeeper called Chimham or Barzillai, and conscious that he was keeping up a tradition almost a thousand years old when he entertained those of David's line? Do not then, imagine a harsh, preoccupied man who missed the great moment of his opportunity, but rather a harassed host who did his best on a night of labour and distress to maintain an ancient rite of hospitality.

13 : The Shepherds and the Emperor

Luke 2.1–20; Micah 5

We have already read Luke's second chapter, but this is a climax of history and we must look at others who crowded that momentous stage. As Paul told the Philippians in quite another context (**3**.1), it is a salutary thing sometimes to be told vital truths more than once.

Stand back like an artist looking at his picture and look again at the story covered by the brief passage of Scripture. Those who looked into the manger at Bethlehem had strange premonitions, but no clear conception of what was to be. The shepherd visitors were a despised and lowly band. The rabbis' literature has words of harsh contempt for their class. And yet it is part of the record of Israel that, when corruption and apostasy invaded high places, faith and truth found fortress and survival among the common folk of the land, the peasantry which sent Elijah and Amos to the courts of wealth and decadence, the people of the ascetic communities, such folk as those of Qumran, who hid their library, the Dead Sea Scrolls, in the wilderness caves . . . It is a pattern which history has seen recur, and in other lands than Palestine.

It was happening in Bethlehem when the hinge of history was turning there. Hillel and Simeon, the proud Pharisees, as we have seen, could actually have been asleep in the inn, with the whole Old Testament stored in their heads. History was passing them by, as it was passing Augustus by in distant Rome, brilliant, able Augustus, his plans for peace and the vital transmission of power frustrated by a restless horse, the sting of an anopheles mosquito, by the invisible invaders of the torrid east, which made fevers mount and wounds inflame. Augustus' heirs fell thus one by one, by accident, wounds, sickness . . .

Augustus was a great man. He had saved his country from the chaos of a hundred years. He had brought order out of the fearsome confusion which had followed the murder of Julius Caesar. He saw hope for the world only in a strong Rome, strongly led, and for a generation now he had ruled wisely and well. He did not know that his census had caused a prophecy to be fulfilled and that a little town in a restless province, not Rome by the Tiber, was at that moment the pivot of history . . . His chosen heirs were dead—Drusus flung from his horse, Gaius and Lucius dead of battle wounds and fever . . . Christ was born.

14 : Men of Bethlehem

John 1.1–18; Luke 19.41–44

Let us stay a little longer in Bethlehem. There were those who came and went and did not know that a tremendous event had taken place. They filled the town, for Rome's bureaucracy had decreed that for census purposes, the people should assemble in the city of their family origin.

Here, for example, is a translation of a public notice, dated A.D. 104. It comes from Egypt, where rainless tracts of desert round the remains of ancient habitation, have preserved from decay masses of written documents from every sphere of human activity. The translation runs:

'Gaius Vibius, chief prefect of Egypt. Because of the approaching census it is necessary for all those residing for any cause away from their own districts to prepare to return at once to their own administrative areas, in order that they may complete the formalities of the family census, so that agricultural land may retain its proper titles. Knowing that your city has need of provisions, I desire . . .'

At this point the document becomes too tattered to read . . . But note the evidence for disrupted food supplies, strained civil amenities, crowded inns . . . And observe why the carpenter of Nazareth and his betrothed wife, both of David's line, were forced, at the command of the bureaucrats, to ride down from Nazareth's lip of hills, across the coloured Esdraelon plain, up through the high country, past Omri's and Ahab's old fortress of Samaria, where collaborator Herod's temple to Augustus was rising, simultaneously with his temple to Jehovah in Jerusalem . . . on through Jerusalem's tangled lanes, over the Mount of Olives, past Bethany, and south to where Bethlehem lay curving on its brown ridge.

'O little town of Bethlehem,' runs the carol, 'how still we see thee lie.' Bethlehem was far from quiet that night. The host who had assembled in a town as old as Genesis seethed with hate for Rome. All the beginnings of Palestine's disaster of eighty years later was there. The men of Bethlehem were Jews we shall meet again, the crowded faces of the story of the Sermon on the Mount, the Galilean seashore, the scene below Pilate's balcony, the slopes of Calvary—and along the invested walls as Titus' legions closed upon the city. They did not know the day of their visitation. They are infinitely pathetic, sheep with no shepherd, and searchers for that which is not bread. They still throng around us—our audience and responsibility.

15 : The Magi

Matthew 2

The common folk found Christ, but so did a few men of intellect, the 'wise men' of another culture, those strange visitants who studied the stars, and followed all the way to

Bethlehem some message they had read in the bright constel-
lations. Tales have gathered round them, for the 'three kings'
do, in fact, illustrate properly how, over the lapse of centuries, a myth can grow. Matthew tells briefly all we really
know. They came, surely, from the Yemen, Arabia Felix, the
land of their gifts, 'gold and frankincense and myrrh'. They
enter the story and leave with mystery behind them. It was
easy enough, from Bethlehem, to connect with the caravan
routes which ran through Petra, and so to avoid returning to
Jerusalem, where the mad king lay in his last evil. They are
symbolic of a longing world-wide, which can be sensed in
page on page of ancient literature, a desire for 'a saviour'.
Misdirected, this yearning led to the worship of Rome's
emperor, the cult of 'the Beast', as the last book of the Bible
puts it, and the long clash with the Church.

History had prepared the path for the Magi. We do not
know how many, over a full thousand years, may have
shared their expectation. Solomon had established relations
with the south-east a thousand years before. His ships went
to Ophir, near modern Aden, and his caravans trod the
desert routes through coloured Petra. Shabwa, ancient Sabota,
was probably the Sheba, whose queen came to see the glory
of Solomon and returned to fill Arabia and Ethiopia across
the strait with legends of her beauty. And Arabia Felix
watched the stars. Her wise men knew their courses. They
worshipped Astarte, who hung in the sky as the Evening
Star, bright as a lamp in the velvet darkness, and often
visible in broad day. Is it not more than possible that with
Judah's cargoes, Judah's Messianic hope went down the
desert ways, and that expectant hearts read the promise
aright even in Arabia Felix? Did not the eunuch of Queen
Candace of Ethiopia come, years later, with his roll of the
prophet Isaiah? And when the time was full, did the glowing
star shine with a new message and draw the Wise Men to
Palestine?

It is a restless, yearning world again, plagued by its own
hates, passions, pride. A scientific age, so rich in the achieve-
ments of its reason, finds it difficult to believe what its eyes
cannot see and its computers measure.

Who are the Wise Men now, when all is told?
   Not men of science; not the great and strong;
   Not those who wear a kingly diadem;

Not those whose eager hands pile high the gold;
But those amid the tumult and the throng
Who follow still the Star of Bethlehem.
(B. Y. Williams)

Questions and themes for study and discussion on Studies 7–15

1. What preparation was God making between the Testaments?
2. In what way did the Old Testament prescribe Christ's ancestry?
3. The influence of Mary in the Christian Church. How should it be recognized?
4. The spiritual blessings of solitude.
5. 'Called to a simple task in an obscure environment.' Should we be content with this?
6. Piety in the midst of poverty.
7. How historical events serve divine ends.
8. The symbolism of the gifts brought by the Magi.

THE WORK OF CHRIST

Redemption in the Old Testament

Though the word 'redemption' is now used as the over-all word for the entire work of Christ, in the Old Testament it has a specific meaning, and generally indicates deliverance on payment of a ransom, as in the case of a slave, or a prisoner of war, or in order to let the condemned go free. In the spiritual sense the Old Testament speaks of God as working out redemption for His people 'with outstretched arm', that is, by the expenditure of energy or the use of power. Thus redemption is always at a cost to the redeemer. Of Christ it is said that we have 'redemption through his blood' (Eph. 1.7).

16: The Cities of Refuge

Numbers 35. 9-28

While redemption means deliverance by means of payment, the nature of the deliverance and the payment make the word cover very diverse areas of human experience.

The establishment of the Cities of Refuge, though initially designed to prevent the outbreak of blood-feud, is illustrative of God's care of human life on occasions of special peril, and of His readiness to cause deliverance to come by means that did not conflict with the demands of justice.

In cases of bloodshed the law of retribution required that the next of kin should be given the duty of avenging the death of his relative. This raised many complications, and a distinction had to be made between wilful murder and accidental homicide. Complicated regulations were therefore drawn up to ensure that the avenger of blood did not act hastily or unjustly as he might well do under a sense of wrong. The fact that in earlier times the unintentional slayer would find sanctuary in the Temple at the altar indicated that God was the protector of his life (1 Kings 1.50 ff.; 2.28-34). Under more settled conditions, when the Temple became established in one place, access to it was not always possible in an emergency. Hence the provision of Cities of Refuge that provided shelter from the avenger of blood. But even in the case of unintentional killing the offender had to endure confinement within the City of Refuge until the death of the High Priest. Some authorities (e.g. the Talmud) hold that this meant that the High Priest took upon himself the responsibility of the accidental death, and so the guilt was expiated in his death.

Even manslaughter broke the Law of God ('you shall not kill'), although, of course, hatred and evil intent made it far more serious. The overall teaching of this provision is that God had a place of protection for the endangered life by which the claims of both justice and mercy were satisfied. It is not difficult to see here a foreshadowing, even at so early a time, of the provision that divine justice and mercy were to make for the protection of the sinner even from the folly of his own sin. Nor is it difficult to go on to claim that the High Priest of our Sanctuary, the Lord Jesus Christ, takes upon Himself the guilt of the sinner, expiates it in His death, and so sets him free. At any rate, the provision accustomed the Israelites to the thought of redemption as God's provision.

17 : Redemption in the Year of Jubilee

Leviticus 25

The institution of the Sabbatical Year follows the pattern of the weekly Sabbath, six years of work followed by a year of rest. When seven Sabbatical Years were concluded, the fiftieth year was recognised as a Year of Jubilee. In either case, it was no empty celebration. In the case of the Sabbatical Year, the land had to have a Sabbath rest and remain uncultivated for a full year. The natural produce of that year was to be free to all and, by God's blessing, it was to be adequate to the needs of all. Some modern practices, such as crop rotation and leasehold have partial resemblance to this idea, although without its religious significance.

The Jubilee Year meant that the rest of the seventh Sabbath Year was extended to one more year, and it was also given an extended significance. It was introduced by the Day of Atonement and was to be a year of liberty and release for person and property. If a Hebrew were sold to a Gentile, or had incurred servitude because of debt, he was to be redeemed by his next of kin, and if that could not be done the servitude ended automatically in the Jubilee Year, and he was free.

Similarly, if land had been sold to a Gentile it must be redeemed by purchase either by the original owner (26) or by the next of kin (25). When that could not be done, it was to revert to its original owner in the Year of Jubilee. Thus Hebrew persons, property, and land came under the law of redemption.

This Sabbatical institution throws further light on the principle of redemption that is latent in the redemption of human beings from the servitude of sin. Not only are their persons delivered, but all with which they are endowed by God shares in the completed redemption. It teaches us that though in Adam we have bartered our patrimony, in Christ we are restored to our lost inheritance, and delivered wholly from the slavery of sin and destruction.

18 : The Redemption from Egypt

Exodus 6.2–9; 15.13–18

Here God reminds Moses of the promises He made to the fathers of the race—Abraham, Isaac and Jacob—and announces that the time of their fulfilment is now at hand (6.2–9). As El-Shaddai—God Almighty—He gave the promises, and now as Yahweh—the faithful Covenant God—He will fulfil them (3). This name was to be an extended revelation of God's character.

Embraced in that Covenant promise was the entire land of Canaan in which their fathers were then only strangers and pilgrims. Now in the fullness of God's time it was to become the possession of their descendants. This involves intervention on their behalf to which God refers as redeeming 'with an outstretched arm' (6). The word 'redeem' carries with it the significance of redemption that we found in our last study, that is, redemption at a cost to the Kinsman-Redeemer.

The divine purpose, however, contained much more than land, it contained a knowledge of God as the Covenant God (6 f.), who was to exercise His power, not only to deliver them from Egypt, but to bring them into Canaan. God Himself is more than His gifts. All this is pledged by the meaning of the Covenant name, again repeated: 'I am the Lord' (8).

Redemption is an experience that makes men sing with joy and praise. When the deliverance from Egypt by the direct intervention of God became a realized fact, Moses had a new vision of the faithfulness of God to which he gave expression in the inspired song sung on the further side of the Red Sea (15.1–21). At v. 13 the faith of Moses already sees the end and the fulfilment of all that had been promised: 'Thou hast led in thy steadfast love the people whom thou hast redeemed, thou hast guided them by thy strength to thy holy abode'; all envisaged as an accomplished fact, even if Canaan and Zion be still far distant in ordinary reckoning, whether it be in terms of years or mileage or sore experience!

The biblical viewpoint is that the exodus from Egypt must rank as an act of divine redemption which foreshadowed the still greater redemption secured by the sacrifice of the Son of God. And the words in which the song of Moses ends are words emblazoned across the redemption of mankind from the Cross to the Crown: 'The Lord shall reign for ever and ever' (18).

19 : The Redemption of the First-Born

Exodus 13.1–16

It is significant that the great event of the deliverance from Egypt was the one selected for a special and perpetual commemoration. This was done in the institution of the Passover Feast. It imposed on all parents a religious duty to tell their children the origin and meaning of the ordinance. For this reason it remained through all the generations, and, in its New Testament counterpart, the Lord's Supper, it shall remain until the Lord's return, a monumental evidence of the authenticity of one of the most stupendous miracles ever recorded in human history.

But what of its claims on the redeemed people? 'Consecrate to me all the first-born' (2), that is, set apart as sacred to God the life that He had spared in Egypt on that night of retribution. The proportion that God demanded, both of the people and of the animals, for His own special service, was the

34

first-born. They bore a special relation to the whole, and, in a sense stood for the whole. The dedication in the case of animals was in the form of sacrifice. Since human sacrifice was not permitted, the first-born of children was to be redeemed, not by a lamb, but with money (Num. 3.46 f.).

Israel was thus to know that redemption makes its claims, and that these must be met in the spirit of sacrifice. While the dedication to God of the first-born was the extent of sacrifice required under the Mosaic Law, under the gospel our entire persons, body, soul and spirit, all we have and all we are, are to be dedicated to the God who has redeemed us (cf. 1 Cor. 6.19 f.). Consider the challenge of that.

20 : The Redemption from Babylon

Isaiah 51.4–11; 52.3–12

The children of Israel were a people with a history. It was their history that led their prophets to believe that what God had done in the past He will still do. The setting of these passages is in Babylon under the conditions of the Jewish captivity. The promise and power of restoration lie in the fact that the captives are 'the redeemed of the Lord', and their deliverance will seem like a new act of redemption in which the sovereign power of God is again felt.

The cry of the captive 'Church' is given in the first passage (51.4–11), and the response of God in the second (52.3–12).

God has promised His captive people that His righteous intervention 'draws near' (51.5), and His people pray to Him to hasten the hour of their deliverance. When that happens the occasion will seem like the awakening of God from sleep, so unconscious are His people of His living power. Reviewing past deliverance and God's unchanging power, they receive new confidence: 'And the ransomed of the Lord shall return, and come to Zion with singing' (11). They remained 'the ransomed of the Lord' even in their state of captivity. It was this relationship that ensured their restoration.

In the second passage, (52.3–12), we have God's response, in which the glorious deliverance of the Jews comes in full sight. His people, prostrate in the dust and ready to die, are awakened at His call. In her folly Judah sold herself into captivity, but she will be redeemed, not by material wealth,

35

but by God's power (3, 6). To prepare for this the captives
have a spiritual duty to fulfil. They must separate themselves
at once from the spiritual conditions of their captivity in a
return to the purity of their ancient faith (11).

The immediate teaching is that the redemption of the Lord
leads to an abiding relationship with Him and this is the
ground of subsequent revival and restoration. Paul finds in
the passage a reference to Christian preaching (Rom. **10**.15),
and a call to the Church of Christ to be separate from the
pollution of the world (2 Cor. **6**.17).

21 : Redemption and Victory over Death

Psalm 49

In this psalm redemption is seen as surviving and overcoming
death. In the setting of worldly aims and ambitions, it contrasts the lot of the wicked and of the righteous, and asserts
the security of the one who trusts in God and not in mere
wealth or temporal prosperity.

This is particularly seen over against the stern reality of
death. In that situation the power of the world's great ones
is as helpless and worthless as that of other men. They cannot
redeem a fellow man from death, or, out of all their wealth,
pay a ransom to the grave for his deliverance (7 ff.).

The impotence of human resources is emphasized in order
to show by contrast the power of the divine ransom. The
redemption of the human soul is 'precious'; it is so costly
that for a mere man to attempt to render it is utter futility (8).

The other side of the contrast is introduced with the words:
'But God' (15). With God on the scene the seemingly futile
and impossible will happen: 'But God will ransom my soul
from the power of Sheol, for he will receive me.' It is not
easy to decide how much we are to understand by this
redemption from Sheol without introducing into it the full
Christian doctrine of the soul's life beyond death and the
resurrection of the body. On the lowest estimate, it must
mean more than the faith that God, in virtue of His redemption, would preserve him from a premature death. In this
context it suggests a reversal after death of human estimates
of a man of God and a man of the world. To be redeemed
or ransomed from the power of the world, or the under-

world of death, suggests the loosening of the hold of death. It is given a further meaning with the words: 'for he will receive me'. This word 'receive' is used of Enoch (Gen. 5.24), and by the psalmist in Psalm 73.24.

It expresses a confidence, we think, that the redemptive power of God will triumph over death. This confidence is based on the fact that the redeemed soul belongs to God in life and death, and that neither death nor the grave can dissolve His claim (cf. Job 19.25). Such an assurance can give new meaning to your life today.

Questions and themes for study and discussion on Studies 16–21

1. In light of the redemption of the Jubilee Year, to what extent do you accept that all our natural endowments, however abused they may have been, may be restored to us in the redemption that is in Christ (Rom. 6.11 ff.; 12.1 f.; Thess. 5.23)?
2. Considering the terms of the Song of Moses on the shore of the Red Sea, what significance do you attach to the term: 'the song of Moses, the servant of God, and the song of the Lamb' (Rev. 15.3)?
3. To what extent, and in what direction, can the Church prepare herself for a spiritual Revival (Isa. 52.11 f., cf. 2 Chron. 7.14; 2 Cor. 6.17)?
4. How do God's redemptive claims constitute the strongest ground for belief in the soul's life beyond death, and the resurrection of the body (1 Pet. 1.18; Rom. 8.23; Phil. 3.21)?

CHARACTER STUDIES

22 : Herod 'The Great'

Matthew 2

When the Romans organized the east in 63 B.C., Pompey appointed a priest named Hyrcanus to rule Galilee, Samaria, Judea, and Perea. Hyrcanus had an astute premier, an Edomite named Antipater, who knew how to use his power for his family's advantage. He secured his two sons, Phasael and Herod, in key governorships, and when Antipater was murdered in 43 B.C., the two young men succeeded jointly to the premiership in Hyrcanus' court.

Phasael was a rapid victim of a Parthian raid which followed the assassination of Julius Caesar, who had intended pacifying that frontier. Herod escaped to Rome and so impressed Octavian, the future Augustus, that he received a mandate to recover Palestine, which he did between 39 and 36 B.C. He successfully carried on a pro-Roman administration for thirty-four years, marked by the building of the Roman port and base at Caesarea and a temple to Augustus at Samaria.

Simultaneously he conciliated the Jews, who hated him for his Edomite blood, by building the great temple at Jerusalem. He was a superb diplomatist, dividing the opposition by suppressing the old aristocracy and yet marrying Mariamne, one of their number, and by setting up a nobility of officials. He stimulated loyalty to his house by founding 'the Herodians', established a strong bureaucracy, secured his power by a mercenary army and a system of strongholds, of which Masada was one, and paid the price of his dangerous living by tension in his own family, murder, and ultimate paranoia.

Herod's private life was soiled by feuds, intrigue and manifold murder. The Emperor Augustus, punning on two Greek words (*hus*—a pig, and *huios*—a son) said he would rather be Herod's pig than his son. As a ruler of the Jews, presumably, he did not keep and kill pigs! He murdered his beloved Mariamne, and at various times three of his sons, one of them in 7 B.C., three years before his death. It is easy to see how the massacre of the children of Bethlehem fits the insane and sanguinary context of Herod's last madly suspicious and ruthless days.

Josephus, the Jewish priest who, as Vespasian's secretary, wrote a history of his people, paints a grim picture of the mental and physical deterioration of the ageing king, prone to delusions of persecution and uncontrollable outbursts of violence, the results of chronic hypertension and a diseased mind. Such was the creature whose evil terrors menaced the cradle of Christ. His common appellation 'the Great' means, in its ancient settings 'the Elder'.

23 : Zechariah

Luke 1.1–25, 57–80; Exodus 30.1–10; Hebrews 10.19–22

The beauty and goodness of this world have always been mingled with its evil and its tragedy. In 'the last days of Herod', when that dark and wicked life was sinking into madness and dissolution, the Remnant we have so often met was still to be found in Israel. It has always been so, from Elijah's seven thousand until today.

The members of Aaron's tribe took it in turn to make the daily sacrifice, and call a blessing on the assembled multitude. We have no information about the surviving numbers of Aaron's descendants, but it may be assumed that the privilege was a rare one and hardly repeated in a man's lifetime. A good man accepted it with awe.

When Zechariah's great day came, he went, no doubt, with deep consciousness of the holy occasion, and a heart prepared to meet his God. God met him in the place of duty, and at the hour of worship. The good man had probably planned to use the great moment at the altar to set before God the burden of his own heart, and he found his burden lifted there. We are always in God's presence. Any moment is our moment of approach. Let us likewise use the privilege.

Voiceless and overwhelmed, Zechariah continued until the task was finished, and gave the people the formal blessing without the customary form of words. They sensed that some great experience had befallen him. It does not need words to show to others that God has touched and sanctified a life. It is too visible in the living presence of a man.

In the last half of the chapter, Zechariah uses his restored speech in praise to God. His hymn is magnificently in character. It is a priest's hymn, alive with references to the Old Testament in which his mind had moved. He had grasped the significance of prophecy, and knew that his son was the forerunner of Christ. He knew as little as his son, even in the climax of his ministry knew, of the true and full significance of the One who was to come, but to fulfil God's plans we do not need fullness of understanding. We need only faithfulness and readiness to act. In humility the committed Christian simply follows step by step and does immediately that which lies closest to the ready hand.

24 : Elizabeth

Luke 1.24, 25, 39–45, 57–63; Psalm 13

Luke has told us, in his opening verses, that he had taken some trouble to verify his facts. He had found aged people still living who remembered old events with all that accuracy with which age remembers the distant past. Elizabeth could have been still alive, high in her eighties. The songs of this chapter may have survived in manuscript. This was a literary age, and preserved its records.

At any rate, we owe it to 'the beloved physician' that these first hymns of the Church were preserved, and that we know a few more of God's remnant. All that was happening in 'the hill country . . . of Judea' (39), was passing the leaders of religion by. If the Pharisees saw nothing in Bethlehem, and if Augustus had not even heard the name, the Sadducees who ruled religion in the land were even further from the truth which might have made them free. The Sadducees denied a resurrection from the dead and rejected the supernatural in religion. They were none the less eager for the emoluments of religion, coveted posts of dignity and the advantages of office, and accepted the profits of the temple court. They are not without posterity.

But return to Elizabeth, warm-hearted, aglow with the new experience of coming motherhood, moved by the strangeness of the events which had preceded that consciousness. How intensely human is the scene in the home of the priest and his wife—the family assembly, the tactless assumption, probably on the part of Elizabeth's parents-in-law, that the father's name would be perpetuated in the son's, and the blank astonishment when the father sided with his wife (63)! The Bible is a book about men and women, as well as about God. God moves through the small affairs of life as well as through the great movements of history. The New Testament often finds its theme where Masefield said he found his poetry. He wrote, he said,

Not of the princes and prelates with periwigged charioteers,
Riding triumphantly laurelled to lap the fat of the years,
But rather the scorned, the rejected, the men hemmed in
with spears.

The Gospels belong to the first century. If we wish to meet the proletariat, the common folk of village, farm, and countryside from that century, there is scarcely anywhere else in surviving literature where modern man may meet them.

25 : Simeon

Luke 2.25–35; Isaiah 42

Joseph, as we have seen, was a man of simple goodness, whose religion consisted in doing that which he ought to do, regardless of the cost, the toil or anything else involved. How desperately the Church, and the tormented world, need such saints.

Certain obligations of the Law (Exod. **13**.12; Lev. **12**.8; Num. **8**.17) brought the necessary outlay within reach of the poor, and the fact that the humble sacrifices were chosen, is indication that no great wealth lay in the hands of Joseph and Mary. Jerusalem was no long journey from Bethlehem, and when Mary could travel, that was the first destination. They passed over the Mount of Olives, in through Saint Stephen's gate, or the gate which was one day to carry that name, and turned left to the Temple. It was a moving moment when the Lord first came to His shrine.

One faithful Israelite was waiting, and recognized the significance of the hour. Faith was still alive in the land, for all the clutter in the temple court, for all the absurdities of Pharisaism. God had his Few. Joseph and Mary, Zechariah

41

and Elizabeth, whom we have already met, were of the number. Simeon was another, and Simeon was led to visit the holy place that day.

Simeon knew the Old Testament, especially Isaiah, and his canticle is a tissue of allusions which show how real to him was messianic expectation (Isa. **40**.3–5; **42**.6; **49**.6; **52**.10). Simeon blessed the parents and, doubtless with the Servant Songs of the ancient prophet in his mind, sounded the note of suffering which was to gather volume in the Messiah's story.

Simeon's blessing, called, from the first words of the Latin version, the Nunc Dimittis, has been part of the daily evening prayers of Western Christendom since the fourth century. It vibrates with gratitude for God's gift to the world, to Israel, and to him.

It was a grand moment for a good man to go. Was he an old man? T. S. Eliot in his *Song for Simeon* makes him one:

Grant us Thy peace.
I have walked many years in this city,
Kept faith and fast, provided for the poor.
Have given and taken honour and ease.
There never went any rejected from my door.

. . . .

Now at this birth season of decease,
Let the Infant, the still unspeaking and unspoken Word,
Grant Israel's consolation
To one who has eighty years and no tomorrow.

No tomorrow? We read of him today—and that is but one kind of immortality.

26 : Anna

Luke 2.36–38; Psalm 71

Another of God's Remnant enters the story, this time an aged woman, but with an insight as keen as that which Simeon had shown. Perhaps she had heard his words of praise and benediction. Old age, as we have more than once seen in these studies, 'hath yet its honour and its toil'. John wrote his Gospel when he was in his nineties. It is a little difficult

42

to calculate Anna's age. Was she eighty-four, or does the phrase (36) mean that she had been a widow after only seven years of married life? If so, she was over a hundred years of age.

She could do little now save give her life to prayer. This does not mean that, at last, with nothing now to occupy her time, she began the ministry of prayer. A lesson worth learning early in life is that, save for the body's weakening, advancing years bring little fundamental change. For good or ill most people are much the same in later life as they are in their middle years and youth. If in her extreme old age, the good woman of the temple court was a person of prayer, it is a fair inference that, all through her life, she had been prayerful.

It is psychological fact that fundamental change becomes more difficult to effect as the years multiply. It is also a fact that, with the amazing triumphs of modern medicine, more people today reach old age than in any generation before. It becomes more relevant, more necessary, to prepare for old age, as the experience of old age becomes more common and more likely. We should bear the fact in mind, deal early with the faults which make old age ugly, learn to be unselfish, to rest in the Lord, not to burden others, to dispense love, to discipline the tongue, to enjoy loneliness, and to live a life of prayer. Anna shows the way. She saw the glory of God in Christ as her reward. Thomas Landels bravely wrote:

And so in looking back at eighty-three
My final word to you, my friends, shall be :
Thank God for life; and when the gift's withdrawn,
Thank God for twilight bell, and coming dawn.

Landels had Tennyson, with whose life he overlapped for thirty years, in mind:

Twilight and evening bell,
*   And after that the dark!*
And may there be no sadness of farewell,
*   When I embark;*
For tho' from out our bourne of time and place
*   The flood may bear me far,*
I hope to see my Pilot face to face
*   When I have crossed the bar.*

27 : Joseph Again

Matthew 2.13–15, 19–23; Hosea 11

Herod's will divided the kingdom which he had ruled so long, so dexterously and so ruthlessly. Archelaus, son of Malthace, a Samaritan woman, took over Judea and Idumea, by far the choicest share. Herod Antipas, son of the same mother, received Galilee and Perea; and Philip, son of a Jewess named Cleopatra, took Iturea, Trachonitis, and the associated territories in the north-east. A map and a Bible atlas are tools of study of some importance. The characters of the Bible lived in time and place. Both time and place, circumstances and habitation, helped to form them and are relevant to our understanding.

Archelaus, who inherited his father's vices without his ability, adopted the title of king, and bloodily quelled disorders which broke out in Jerusalem. The result was a wider uprising, which required the strong intervention of Varus, the governor of Syria. These were the troubled circumstances which Joseph was led to avoid. He probably took the road up through the coastal plain, over the famous Megiddo Pass, where Josiah fell (2 Kings 23), across the Plain of Esdraelon, and up the hills to Nazareth. Archelaus' stupid rule continued till A.D. 6, when Jewish protest secured his banishment.

Amid these stormy events Joseph trod his careful way. No one who saw the little party moving north with their few poor possessions could imagine that the man with the bag of carpenter's tools was the frail custodian of God's plan. The Messiah was coming home, repeating, Matthew's pious thought saw, in symbolic form, the old story of the Exodus. The family settled in the town on the ridge of hills which forms the southern rampart of Galilee, a place not mentioned in the Old Testament, but bearing a name which suggested a verse in Isaiah (11.1), where Christ is spoken of as a *netzer* (that is a *sprout* or a *shoot*) from the stem of Jesse. This is a type of mystical exegesis not familiar to our mind, but part of the Hebrew habit of thought, and valid as a sign to those who thus used their ancient Scriptures.

Joseph had no such thoughts as he plodded the weary miles up from Egypt. He had walked far for Mary's Son, and God had paid his way, for gold was one of the gifts the Magi brought. He was a good man, and in this chapter, his work

44

done, he passes from the page of history. In the chapel of the hospital in Nazareth today, stands for an altar a carpenter's bench, the working side turned towards the congregation. Joseph was glad to set up his bench in Nazareth and prepare to provide for the Christ.

28 : The Child Jesus

Luke 2.41–52; Deuteronomy 16.1–8

The picture of the family from Nazareth, journeying faithfully to Jerusalem for the Passover feast, is a revealing one. They appear also to have remained in the city for the full length of the festival. There may have been a special reason for this visit. A Jewish boy was accounted of responsible age at twelve years, when he was said to become 'a son of the Law'. There would be some ceremony in the Temple, or in a synagogue near the Temple in which dress proper to the boy's maturity would be given, and appropriate exhortation made. It was a solemn and impressive occasion.

The caravan set out for home, in all probability by the northern hill-road, which ran up through Samaria, relatives and townsfolk travelling together to guarantee security. This is how the Child's absence remained unnoticed all through the first day's travelling. The anxious couple took a whole day to travel back, and on the third day, after visiting their late lodgings, went to the Temple and encountered a strange sight. The boy sat in the most august company.

There are several legends of Jesus' childhood and infancy, dating from the second century, and full of fantastic details. This story, rescued from oblivion by the diligent Luke, and bearing the freshness of Mary's own telling, rings true. Jesus sat with the teachers of the Law, astonishing them by the maturity of His understanding. With His new garments, a new dignity seemed to rest on Him. Joseph and Mary must have felt, from this day on, that there was a part of Him which they were unable convincingly to penetrate.

Mary 'kept all these things in her heart'. One can almost hear her telling Luke the story. Something utterly amazed them. Joseph was too abashed to speak in such a company. Mary spoke out in her motherly concern and relief, and

45

received a strange answer: 'Did you not know that I would be in my Father's house?'

He returned with them to Nazareth, and almost another twenty years of life are summed up in the phrase: 'he was obedient to them'. He Himself obeyed, and in the process grew up, a true man beloved of men, beloved of God (52).

Questions and themes for study and discussion on Studies 22–28

1. How many Old Testament references can be identified in the psalms of Luke?
2. How do Luke's opening chapters in other ways link the Testaments together?
3. How does Paul support the doctrine of the Virgin Birth (Rom. 5; 1 Cor. 15)?
4. Who ultimately make history—the good or the powerful?
5. Meeting in the place of service.
6. List the Remnant as they appear in the opening chapters of the Gospels.
7. Waiting for God's revelation. Is there still something to wait for?
8. The usefulness of the old.
9. Obedience as Joseph illustrates it.

THE WORK OF CHRIST

Suffering in the Old Testament

The problem of suffering was as deep a mystery to the people of the Old Testament as it is to us today. Especially was this so with respect to what they regarded as 'unmerited suffering'. It is apparent, however, that in the Old Testament suffering often has a reference beyond mere personal experience. It may be vicarious. Good men, whose righteous character provoked the hostility of others, and whose calling was to represent the redemptive purpose of God to Israel, often felt drawn into depths of suffering that put them into sympathy with the Ideal Sufferer yet to come. Though their sufferings and laments may have had, in the first instance, reference to their own circumstances, they seem suddenly to be drawn into circumstances beyond their own. This is what the New Testament, speaking of Christ, calls 'the fellowship of his sufferings' (Phil. 3.10).

29: The Suffering Servant

Psalm 22

This has been called 'a psalm of sobs'. While much of it could be the experience of the psalmist himself, there are details that can hardly have been part of his own experience (cf. v. 16). For this and other reasons it has been given a prophetic setting and made applicable, in the fullest sense, to the Ideal Sufferer of prophetic history, the Messiah of Israel. As an expression of personal suffering viewed through the eyes of the sufferer himself, it is perhaps unique in Old Testament literature. It is not suffering in general, but the suffering of a certain person who is giving vent to ejaculations of personal pain.

Note these points in his sufferings:

Its loneliness (1, 2). The acute consciousness of being alone in his distress accentuates his sufferings. The denial of God's

47

presence and refusal to answer his cry is the sorest ingredient (cf. Mark 15.34).

Its humiliation (6–8). In his sense of desertion he feels more abject than any human being, a mere worm to be trampled on, and an object of reproach to passers-by who cast aspersions on the reality of his trust in God (cf. Matt. 27.43).

Its publicity (12–18). Suffering humanity asks for privacy, and this is granted in death even to wild animals. But this man is asked to suffer and die in the full glare of publicity. This reaches its unbearable climax in v. 17.

Its violence (16). Even his body was not spared in the hour of his distress. His hands and feet were pierced or torn.

His sufferings, however, are vicarious, for they bring the people back to God, extend His Kingdom, manifest His just government, and make the righteous judgements of God known to posterity (22–31).

We feel that Jesus Christ alone can fit fully into this pattern of personal suffering. He must have found it so, for He made it an expression of His feelings while He hung on the Cross. The words 'he has wrought it' (31) may have found expression in the cry, 'It is finished' (John 19.30), suggesting perhaps that He repeated the psalm from first to last.

30 : Suffering and Faith in God

Psalm 69

This is a further expression of suffering attributed to David, and yet, as in Psa. 22, not exhausted in David's own experience. For that reason it is transferred to the Ideal Sufferer and so quoted in several passages of the New Testament (John 2.17; 15.25; Acts 1. 20; Rom. 11.9 f.; 15.3). The features of the suffering may be noted as follows:

Afflicted innocence (1–4). The imagery is that of an inner sorrow: the waters, the mire, the flood, are expressions of a mental and spiritual experience. The general hatred of which he is the target is 'without cause' (4), and under this reproach he made compensation for what he had been wrongfully accused of appropriating (4).

Righteous suffering (6–12). While he is anxious that his friends should not be involved in the suffering which he bears because of his faithfulness to God, he is very conscious that his godliness is the reason for their mockery (6–9). His friends have forsaken him and his enemies add inhuman harshness to their reproaches (10 f.).

Acute sensitivity (11–21). He shudders at the insults heaped upon him: to the mockery ('I become a byword'), to the derision (the song of the drunkard), until at last the reproach breaks his heart (20).

From this condition faith sees a glorious outcome (30–36). Here emphasis is placed on the future as faith sees it: truth will be exalted, the salvation of God will be exhibited, and the spirit of worship fostered.

We may see both David and Christ in this particular expression of suffering. As all of it could not have been applicable to David historically, so all of it is not applicable to Christ. But its anticipations of Christ's sufferings have been so fully fulfilled in the Gospel narratives of the crucifixion that only the prophetic spirit bestowed on David could have received and conveyed them.

31 : Job in Suffering

Job 29 and 30

In the person of Job we have suffering depicted against the background of former prosperity and power. His former greatness is still fresh in Job's memory: his comfort in his religion and his family, the respect paid to him by his fellow men, and the good that he had been able to render to the afflicted when he had the means of doing so (ch. **29**).

It is in the light of all this that he views his present misery and feels its sting (ch. **30**).

His sufferings come from three directions:

They are from without (1–15). He is insulted by men whom he had befriended and helped: men, with no name and no honour, now 'spit at the sight' of him (10). He becomes the target of their jibes and contempt (9). To add to his bitter-

ness, this treatment is meted out to him in his physical afflic-
tion and outward misfortunes, when he most needed kindness
and comfort.

They are from within (16–18, 30). His soul 'poured out'
within him is the expression of his inner anguish. Verse 17
vividly expresses his unrelieved physical torment.

They are from above (19–23). He traces the hand of God
in all that is happening to him. It is God that casts him in
the mire (19), and refuses to answer his desperate cry (20).
He sums it up in the terrible outburst addressed to God:
'Thou hast turned cruel to me' (21). Even death that he would
welcome does not come to him.

Though it is clear that God assigned to Job 'the ministry
of suffering' because He trusted and loved him, there are
depths in it that we cannot plumb. But it is difficult to avoid
a comparison between the nature and intensity of his sufferings, and those of the suffering Messiah of Israel. Indeed,
the historical narrative of Calvary would suggest at some
points a striking parallel. In Christ's consciousness His
enemies acted with divine permission (John 19.11). And His
sufferings must be viewed against the background that lent
such pungency to Job's experience. Paul expressed it thus:
'For you know the grace of our Lord Jesus Christ, that
though he was rich, yet for your sake he became poor, so
that by his poverty you might become rich' (2 Cor. 8.9).

32 : Jeremiah under Suffering

Jeremiah 11.18–23; 20.1–18

Jeremiah brings to light the price, in terms of suffering, that
he had to pay for his fidelity to God. In this context, he may
be said to enter into sympathy with the Ideal Sufferer of
prophecy.

He charges his people, who were of the priestly house of
Abiathar, with unfaithfulness to God's command, and
threatens them with disaster for their idolatry. So desperate is
their spiritual condition that the prophet is forbidden to pray
for them (11.14). God has pronounced judgement on them,
and at His command the Chaldeans have kindled the fire for
their destruction.

In return for his faithfulness in exposing their sins and declaring God's judgements Jeremiah discovers that a conspiracy is formed against him by his priestly brethren, the men of Anathoth (19). It was a conspiracy to destroy him, for nothing short of his blood would satisfy them.

God disappoints their hopes by revealing to the prophet his danger. He realizes that as a lamb or an ox he was being brought to the slaughter (18, 19), and he appeals to God to settle the matter with them since he was unwilling to take vengeance into his own hands. The divine judgement is destruction by famine and sword (22 f.).

In ch. **20** we see Jeremiah falling again into the hands of the priestly class; Pashhur flogged him, and imprisoned him for one day. But he utterly failed to prevent Jeremiah from giving his message of coming judgement and of his death as a captive in Babylon. Furthermore, the fortifications of Jerusalem would be razed to the ground, and the royal treasures taken to Babylon (cf. Matt. **24**.2). The man of God is no opportunist.

The price of fidelity is not merely physical suffering, it is often a surge of depression that overwhelms the faithful servant (**20**.7 ff.). Jeremiah is tempted to think that God has failed to protect him. Verse 7 can equally well be translated: 'Thou hast persuaded me and I was persuaded', that is, he yielded to a divine compulsion, and the promised results did not seem to come. But the fire of prophecy was burning within, and Jeremiah could not restrain the urge. By submission he tested the faithfulness of God in the end of the day.

The experience of Jeremiah proclaims the sufferings that must come to the faithful witness. To that extent his suffering sheds light on the experience of Jesus Christ, 'the faithful witness' (Rev. **1**.5), and of all who 'suffer for righteousness' sake' (Matt. **5**.10; 1 Pet. **3**.14).

33 : The Vocation of Suffering

Isaiah 50.4–9

This is the third of the 'Servant passages' in Isaiah's prophecy, the first and second being **42**.1 ff. and **49**.1 ff. There is only one Person who fits perfectly into all these passages, even if at times He transcends them. He is not Cyrus, but the Lord Jesus Christ. The service that Christ was to perform in obedience to His Father's will entailed suffering, and in Him the Ideal Sufferer of many another passage—whether it be of sacrifice, or type, or promise—comes so fully to view that, in instant recognition, we cry: 'It is the Lord'. From this passage we learn that He had, not only to be appointed to the endurance of suffering, but endowed and equipped for its ministry. With Him it was a vocation, and His teacher was His Heavenly Father (4).

Note that Christ was given a sensitivity to suffering that enabled Him to instruct and comfort the 'weary'. For this He had to live in unbroken communion with the mind and will of God (4, cf. John **8**.29).

He also had the spirit of instant obedience that refused to yield either to fear or to rebellion, even at the disclosure of the ordeal awaiting Him.

He had the spirit of meekness that led Him to face the horror of physical and spiritual assaults with quiet submission (6, cf. John **18**.8).

Conscious of God's help He had the courage and resolution to carry on to the end, fully confident that God would sustain Him and eventually vindicate His cause (7, cf. Luke **9**.51). No matter how great his sufferings He knew that no one could ultimately overcome Him (8 f.).

All this serves to unfold the voluntary nature of the Servant's sufferings, and His willing acceptance of the path that was to lead to the Cross. He knew from the beginning what the programme of redemption involved for Him, and He accepted it as the will of His Father (John **18**.11).

34 : Vicarious Suffering

Isaiah 52.13–53.12

Our immediate interest in this passage is that the waters of redemption which, as we have already seen, course through the whole of the Old Testament, through symbol and sacrifice, here come so near the surface that we can hear the joyful sound (Psa. **89**.15 AV), and see the fountain opened for sin (Zech. **13**.1). We are entering here more fully into suffering that is vicarious, the one for the many. Chapter **53** is deservedly called 'Isaiah's Golden Passional'.

The passage we now study would seem to look at the sufferings of the Servant from three different aspects, presenting three different assessments.

(1) God presents the theme and gives a summary of the work of the Servant that serves as an introduction to all that is to follow (**52**.13–15). It is a presentation of suffering and triumph still to come, and this note is struck twice in the passage. That God's Servant would 'prosper' in His undertaking is perhaps too mild a translation of a remarkable word which bears the idea of intelligent forethought, as of the farmer who sows his seed in the spring with the intelligent expectation of the harvest he will reap (cf. John **12**.24). It suggests the cold, damp earth of spring followed by the golden fields of harvest. Then again, the unattractive appearance of the Servant (14) has its unexpected sequel in His royal exaltation (15), truly a 'startling' reversal of fortune that will arrest universal attention.

The introductory future tense used in the passage here sets the time of the entire happening: vivid as the portrayal is, the event is still in the future.

(2) Next comes the assessment and verdict of unbelief (**53**.1–3). The prophet recognizes that his message of a suffering Saviour met with incredulity and rejection (1). To unbelief the Sufferer is but as a frail sapling ready to perish, or as a shrivelled root already half-dead. For that reason, He is not only unattractive, He is despised and rejected, so abhorrent that men turn away their faces from Him (3).

(3) The vision and assessment of faith is now given (4-9). There is an acknowledgment that when He was seen bearing the sorrows of others, it was attributed by men to divine punishment meted out to Him because of His own sin (4). But now we—the personal note is the only one that is appropriate—relate it all to our sins (5), and we are driven to penitent confession (6). When we saw Him so overwhelmed with suffering and sorrows, we thought this was the end of Him (8). So did His tormentors, who had planned His grave with the robbers who died at His side. But there was a divine intervention, and He was buried in a rich man's grave (cf. Matt. **27**.57). The penalty of sin was carried by Him, and the victim was delivered for the reason given in v. 9.

53

There is now a return to the scene by the Supreme Judge who presided over it all, and He gives the final assessment (10–12). It was the Lord who bruised Him as Sin-bearer (10). This suggests that His most intense sufferings were spiritual, not merely physical. But the righteous Judge will see to it that His reward is commensurate with His sufferings (12). For Paul's commentary on this read Phil. 2.8 ff.

It is practically impossible to put any other case of suffering into this passage but the suffering of Jesus Christ in life and death, and none other triumph but that of His resurrection and eternal reign. As far as the portrayal of personal suffering goes, to us now it is history rather than prophecy.

Questions and themes for study and discussion on Studies 29–34

1. How would you relate the general experience of personal suffering to the purpose of life?

2. It has been said of Job: 'Of all men he was the one fitted most to be entrusted with the service of suffering'. How true is this?

3. It has been said that, while the four Gospels give us the biography of Christ, it is the psalms that give His autobiography. Would you justify this as far as Pss. **22** and **69** are concerned?

4. What significance would you attach to the fact that Christ, though in His sufferings 'numbered with the transgressors' (Isa. **53**.12), was in His death not placed in a malefactor's grave?

5. To what extent is the kingly power of Christ mediated to us through His sufferings? (See 'therefore' in Isa. **53**.12 and in Phil. **2**.9).

CHARACTER STUDIES

35 : The Rulers

Luke 3.1, 2; Psalms 93 and 110

Like the meticulous historian that he was, Luke pinpoints the moment of John's desert ministry, and we meet a cluster of characters, only some of whom we shall meet again in the New Testament. We shall meet the sinister Herod and the scheming priest Caiaphas.

Save for the moment when his face, stamped on a silver denarius, lay in the open hand of Christ, and save for his name called in threat and protest by the priests and their minions at the trial of the Lord, the second emperor of Rome, the dour Tiberius, will not appear again.

Tiberius was born in 42 B.C. He died in A.D. 37. He succeeded to the principate in A.D. 14, on Augustus' death, when he was fifty-six years of age. He was now over seventy. Tiberius was a deeply embittered man when he became Rome's ruler. He was Augustus' stepson, and disliked by the Emperor. Augustus did his best to find an heir to the principate more congenial to his taste, but was dogged by cruel misfortune all along the line of his endeavours. Again and again his successor-designate, or some youth groomed for that exalted position, died tragically, and in the end, anxious for the preservation of the Roman Peace of which he was the architect, Augustus reconciled himself to Tiberius.

It was too late to save a personality naturally dour, suspicious, cold and withdrawn, from the wounds and damage of such humiliation and rejection. Tiberius was an able man, and research has done much to rescue his memory from the grim reputation which the brilliance of the historian Tacitus fastened upon it. But Tiberius was the type of man on whom evil rumour seems naturally to fasten. He was now in retirement on Capri, watchful, bitterly suspicious and dangerous. That is why Pilate feared him.

But such was the background in the wide world where

history, or so men thought, was made, when the Baptist lifted up his voice in the Jordan wilderness. No one imagined that the most deeply significant events of that year were made, not in Rome, nor yet in the small province where Philip, best of old Herod's three sons, exercised his authority, nor where Herod Antipater (Antipas), following his father's clever diplomatic policy with precarious deviations, managed to carry on, at least through these years, his puppet rule. It is difficult, in any year, to know where the true significance of history lies. Perhaps some hope lies there.

36 : John, Heir of Elijah

Malachi 3.1–6; 4.5, 6; Mark 1.1–11

In his brisk business-like way Mark speaks of a fulfilment of an ancient prophecy in the ministry of John the Baptist. The other three evangelists speak of this event at greater length and we shall look more closely at this Elijah-like character in the next two studies. Mark stresses in his brief account that John's ministry was a ministry of the wilderness, and in the fact lies a clue to the character of the man who led the great revival in Judea which prepared the way for the coming of Christ.

John's preaching-place was the wide river valley of the lower Jordan. Some touch of God on heart and mind made John aware of a divine calling, and he was haunted by the figures of Elijah, Elisha and Isaiah. The two earlier prophets were both associated with the Jordan. Elijah, as his ministry ended, felt himself drawn to that river frontier by which Israel had first entered the land, and over which he himself had come from Gilead, when he first burst upon the court of Ahab.

Here it was that Elijah, like Moses, went his way, and his spirit fell upon Elisha. It is easy to read John's mind. He knew the strange verse in Malachi which ended the canon of the Old Testament. The deep conviction was upon him that he was to begin something new. He sought the old places of bestowal and revelation. That tortuously winding stream, Israel's only river, had been marked by the giving of the Spirit, and the symbolic washing of water, for it was to the Jordan that Elisha had sent Naaman, sacramentally to bathe his leprosy away.

History can be a strong and living force. Christianity, like Judaism, is based and rooted in the historic events of a revelation. This is what John instinctively knew, and it was history which he drew from that strange landscape, the vast trench with the wide, green jungle-floor between the arid uplands of Judea where he was born and the tall ramparts of the mountains of Moab on the far side, the walls of the wilderness whence Israel had come, and the bastions of her enemies.

Hence qualities of character which made the Forerunner what he was. Hence the need for Christians to know and to savour their own historic past. That is why these notes turn from character to character in the Bible. We shall meet no prophet greater than John.

37 : John the Preacher

Matthew 3.1–17; Luke 3.1–20

Down the long twisting miles from Jerusalem, high on its ridge, to the valley floor, deep below sea level, came the multitudes to hear the preaching of John. His stern, terse words again reveal the man and his training. The wild environment gave him his imagery and illustration. It was the wet shingle in the river-bed to which he pointed when he said that God could of the very stones raise up children to Abraham. And there was woodcutting in the Jordan jungle, to provide the word picture of the aimed and ready axe. Where there is woodcutting there is also the scrub-fire, such as Moses saw in Sinai. Before the flames the pests of the undergrowth, the vipers and scorpions, fled.

But it was the prophet Isaiah, as we shall see especially in John's account, that provided the Baptist with the core of his message, and perhaps there is another pointer here to a further influence upon his life. Not far from the traditional place of baptism is the Dead Sea, and round the north-eastern curve of that sea's arid shore lay Qumran, best known, thanks to recent archaeology, of the haunts of the wilderness sects.

It is a fair inference from the place of his ministry that John had spent long years of training and preparation in the desert. It is not impossible that he could have found refuge in such communities as that of Qumran although he drifted from them theologically. We know something of the library of Qumran, for when, in the Great Rebellion of A.D. 66 to 70, the Roman patrols quenched all guerrilla opposition in the Jordan valley, the folk of Qumran hid their precious scrolls in the cliff-side caves.

Perhaps their most prized book was a magnificent scroll of the prophet Isaiah. It was certainly in existence in John's day, and may have been the very book which John studied, with the six-centuries-old oracles coming to life in his mind. John preached repentance, in the sterner terms of the Old Testament, perhaps, than with the grace and persuasion proper to the New, but preaching for a verdict, for decision and committal, is as relevant today as it was when John cried aloud in the Jordan wilderness. There is no other way to prepare the way of the Lord than by repentance.

38 : John and his Visitors

Matthew 11.1–15; John 1.6–34

John was not the man to waste his time on those not there truly to listen. The interview with the delegation from the Sanhedrin is told in a manner typical of the fourth evangelist's reporting. Observe the laconic answer given to the blunt question put to him (19 f.). In the Greek text the words are even more abrupt than the translation makes them, and the Greek text no doubt reflects the Aramaic of the riverside conversation.

The delegates were, in fact, discourteous. Such questions are not directed bluntly in the East. Witness Nicodemus' courteous preamble in his interview with the Lord. Reading the question to which the priests were leading, John anticipated their words with a denial to all claims to be the Messiah. He said nothing more, for no one is under obligation to answer malign and loaded questions. In the next verse (21) crude discourtesy is apparent. 'What, then?' they say, not 'Who?'

John does not reply, so they proceed: 'Are you Elijah?' He denies it. There was a mystic sense in which John was to be regarded as Elijah, but he was replying with crushing brevity to a question intended to compromise him, and his answers are more and more sparing of words. At last (22) the officious delegation see the need for courtesy. They have come to a point at which they begin to fear for the success of their mission. After all, they have been sent by the hierarchy to make certain specific enquiries, and could be in an awkward position if it was to become clear that unauthorized rudeness of their own invention had spoiled all chance of a proper reply.

Given a correct approach, John replies with words of Old Testament Scripture. He rested on the Word, and such were the beliefs and preoccupations of the Pharisees that, on that ground, he was safe. It was skilful debating of the sort the Lord Himself, in similar contexts, was to demonstrate. He continued with his proclamation—that his function was simply to prepare the way.

John adapted his message to each group which approached him, as may be specially seen in Luke's account. Sin, and consequently repentance, finds first expression in the immediate environment, and the nearest confrontation with the Enemy. This was soon to be shown in the temptation of Christ.

39 : The Tempter

Matthew 4.1–11; Genesis 3.1–13; Romans 8.35–39

We have met the Tempter, the Mind behind Evil, before. Jesus had waited, it appears, until the mass movement of John's revival was past. He sought no spectacular publicity. John had known his relative as a man of God, and paid Him a splendid tribute. Then came the sign from God. John's mind had moved in the thought, language and imagery of the great Isaiah, and Isaiah had cried in stress of soul: 'O that Thou wouldst rend the heavens and come down' (64.1). So it came to pass, and a new page of history began. The Messiah stepped out on His ministry.

He was never more a human character of the Bible than

at that moment when, needing no repentance, He nevertheless took His place beside sinful men at the place of baptism. And as so often seems to happen in the experience of
men, the challenge was accepted by the Tempter. He had
gone away to keep a lonely vigil and to face the vast issues
which now confronted Him. He left the river bank, and
walked back perhaps in the direction of the most ancient
city in the land, the old Canaanite stronghold of Jericho.

Today Jericho lies on the green valley floor not vitally
different from the Jericho of the first century, save that the
mauve flowered jacaranda has joined the palms and cypress
for which the town was famous. Nearby, in and under an
ancient ruin-mound, lie the remnants of old fortifications
which the archaeologists untangle, and which go back to the
dawn of history.

A mile back from the mound stands a harsh steep mass
of arid rock, a deserted wilderness of hidden tracks and
caverns, where the loneliness and barrenness of a thirsty land
could be felt. There went Christ. There went the Tempter. It
is the way with him to await the lonely moment. Alone the
Lord faced the problems of His ministry—the hungry multitude, the proud capital eager for a sign, the alien, and other
nations. There was a carnal answer and a spiritual answer in
each case. The Tempter suggested the former and ham-
mered the beleagured mind for forty days. In tomorrow's
reading from Luke it will be seen that the order of the three
temptations is varied. The Tempter knows well how to make
his thrusts repetitive, varied, infinitely subtle in their probing
for the weak point in the wall, organizing the attack, ambush,
storming, sabotage, switching the pressure now here, now
there . . .

40 : The Tempted

Luke 4.1–13; Hebrews 2.16–18; 4.12–16; 1 Corinthians 10.12, 13

In this awesome scene we look at One who had no sin but
was tempted in every way which is common to man—along
the line of the body's natural needs and appetites, along the

line of spectacular service, and through the imagination, firing laudable ambition. Here is Everyman but also Perfect Man, facing the storm and stress of every day.

There is, of course, no mountain in the world from which all the world's kingdoms can be overlooked together. This was a thrust at the soul's citadel through the memory. The story is using a metaphor without acknowledgement, as Eastern speech so often does. In His youth and boyhood Jesus must often have climbed to the lip of the ridge of hills above Nazareth. Beneath, running west and north to the rampart of Carmel, is the plain of Megiddo, sprawling, in Jacob's phrase, 'like an ass', among the spurs of surrounding hills. This is the northern door to Palestine. All history has marched south and north this way. Here came Sisera. Yonder Gideon's commandos lay. This way, earlier still, journeyed Abraham. Assyrians and Babylonians had poured along the same road into the cockpit of the East. Alexander brought his Macedonians, Pompey the eagles of Rome, along this path. Future history was to be just as full. Vespasian, Omar, Saladin, Napoleon, Allenby, all knew the plain beneath the hills of Nazareth. It was a stage of empire. A boy's vivid mind might well have seen the vision of 'the kingdoms of the earth' below this native village. And now in the Temptation a dream of youth comes flooding back. These armies, these peoples. He could rule them. Rule them! And then He saw the Via Dolorosa and the Cross—and chose the Cross.

The character of the Tempted One, at this critical moment in time, is worth watching for its response. The Lord answered with the Word. For weeks, while the grim struggle lasted, He threw back each plausible and twisted argument with Scripture. Such is the safe reply. We must have objective standards, and they must be founded on authority. In stress of mind and body under the varied assault of evil, the Sword of the Spirit is the only trusty blade.

Questions and themes for study and discussion on Studies 35–40

1. Christianity's foundation in history. Is it important?
2. In what way did John fulfil Malachi's prophecy?
3. The role of the wilderness in Hebrew history.

4. Why is repentance vital?
5. Is John a model for the preacher?
6. Why was Christ baptized?
7. Why was Christ tempted?
8. The Bible and temptation.
9. Is loneliness a good thing?

THE WORK OF CHRIST

The Teaching of Jesus

It seems true that our Lord did not want to disclose fully the nature of His saving work until it was complete. It required the Cross, the Resurrection and Pentecost to shed further light on His mission so that the way of salvation could be made clear to us. Nevertheless, however much we learn from other sources, it must all be rooted in the self-disclosure of Christ given to us in the Gospels. For that reason, the four Gospels, presenting to us the mind of Christ, must be our primary source of knowledge regarding His mission into the world to seek and to save lost mankind.

41 The Bridegroom Taken

Luke 5.33–6.11

The work of Christ derives its meaning and authority from the teaching of Jesus Himself. This passage is important as marking Christ's final break with the Pharisees and His first public intimation, albeit veiled, of His death (but cf. the hint to Nicodemus privately, John 3.14). And He did it, characteristically, in a figure that high-lighted, not His own deprivation, but that of His disciples.

Note what He means by the friends of the bridegroom being deprived. In reply to the charge that His disciples lacked the devout and ascetic habits of the disciples of John and of the Pharisees, Christ used an illustration drawn from an Eastern wedding. The friends of the bridegroom remained with him throughout the seven days of the festive celebrations. When at the end of the period the bridegroom departed, the fellowship broke up and the joy was turned into sadness.

In applying this to the existing relations between Himself and His disciples, Christ indicated an abrupt ending to the fellowship when the Bridegroom would be forcibly taken away. The word translated 'taken away' is used only here

and in Matthew's and Mark's accounts of the same event—
and it hints at a violent end to the fellowship. It was undoubtedly in Christ's mind to disclose that the fellowship
with His disciples would be abruptly and violently terminated
by His death at the hands of His enemies.

This teaching was followed by two illustrations of the
folly of mixing the old forms of Judaism with the spirit of
the new life introduced by Christ (36–39). Note that the old
wine, that is, the old forms of religion, was pronounced
'good', with the undertone of 'best', by those who had refused to drink of the new! This is of the essence of prejudice.

The relevance to our subject of the other two incidents—
the conduct of the disciples, and the healing miracle of
Christ, both done on the Sabbath day—is that they widened
the breach between Christ and the Pharisees. This resulted
in a determination on the part of the Pharisees that He must
be destroyed rather than have their authority challenged by
His conduct. Henceforward this determination became the
motivating principle of their attitude to Jesus.

It is significant that in what has been called 'the Galilean
spring-time' of the ministry of Jesus, there is this cloud in
His sky and this presentiment of His death breaking through.
From this time onwards it can be seen that it was scarcely
ever absent from His thoughts.

42 : The Bread of Life

John 6.35–71

This address was given in the synagogue of Capernaum
where Jesus was well-known from His early ministry (42).
He proclaimed to all within hearing the fact that now occupied so much of His thoughts, that He was to die, and that
life would emerge from His death.

He presented Himself as 'the bread of life', using the
analogy of the manna provided for the Israelites in the
wilderness. The similarity was not as disturbing to His hearers as the contrast, for He also claimed that He was the
true bread from heaven (50, cf. v. 32).

Fully aware that this gave offence to the religious leaders,
He proceeded to identify Himself as the source and agent

of the resurrection or eternal life (44 ff.). The offence was aggravated when He indicated that this divine life found in Him was made available to men only because He would die (55 f.). He revealed this under the startling figure of making His flesh and blood the spiritual food of all who believed in Him, claiming at the same time that this life, arising from His death, was available to the whole world (51). When He refers to this as still future, it shows clearly that He meant that His approaching death would make Him available to all men.

Many were now offended even within the group of His followers as they fastened on the mysterious figure of His flesh being food for them (52). They found it a 'hard saying' — rough and offensive—and gave up following Him (66). Consequently, Jesus turned to His immediate followers, the twelve disciples presenting them with the challenge: 'Will you also go away?' Simon Peter would seem to have answered for all of them when he avowed allegiance to Jesus as Messiah and the Giver of eternal life (68 f.). Christ's reply was as revealing as it was unexpected. For the first time He disclosed to His disciples His knowledge of the events that would reach their climax in His death, and that one of them should turn traitor.

This disclosure put Jesus consciously at the very heart of the events that would culminate in His crucifixion. It is obvious now that to Him death was not His fate, as in the case of all other men, it was His deed (John **10**.17). Clearly, He was in possession of the programme that was unfolding.

43 : The Disclosure at Caesarea Philippi

Mark 8.27–9.1, 30–32

The confession of Peter on the journey through Caesarea Philippi (**8**.29) occupies an important place in the earthly career of Jesus. Especially is this so as it formed the background to the most complete disclosure of His sufferings, death, and resurrection that He had yet given publicly. Before this Christ had avoided any public disclosure, as it might precipitate action on the part of both His friends and His enemies, though in different directions.

Peter's rebuke to his Master (32) indicates how far His

disciples were from understanding the programme of suffering, rejection and death on which He was embarking. Peter's
reluctance to accept this, Christ attributes to Satanic influence that would suggest an easier way, and so thwart the
redemptive purpose of God (cf. Luke 4.5–8).

The implications of His rejection and death for His followers in every age—and therefore for us—were clearly understood by Christ as involving self-denial, suffering and cross-
bearing (34). The Cross of Christ, indeed, brought to light a
law of the spiritual life: only in self-giving can life have its
richest fulfilment (35). For His followers, in particular, the
renunciation of personal ambition, and the denial of self at
whatever personal cost, was the price of true discipleship
(38).

Christ's further disclosure (9.1), that the Kingdom of God
would 'come with power' in the experience of some of His
disciples, found fulfilment after six days when He took Peter,
James and John to the Mount of Transfiguration. That, in the
experience of the three disciples, was an outstanding example
of the Kingdom of God—the spiritual realm to which Christ
so often referred as the great spiritual reality behind the
present and temporary—breaking through. There on the
Mount the veil between the seen and the unseen was rent,
and the representatives of the Old Testament Church—Moses
and Elijah—were conferring with Christ about the coming
death at Jerusalem. This was, apparently, of absorbing interest
to both Heaven and earth (Luke 9.31).

Two thoughts are suggested by this study. First, how far
the minds of the disciples were from being conditioned by
Christ's teaching to predispose them to accept the Cross and
the resurrection when these took place. And second, how
clearly Christ Himself saw beforehand the entire course of
events of which He was to be the centre.

44 : Entering the Cloud

Mark 10.32–45; Luke 12.49–53

On this the last journey to Jerusalem, the Master's unusual
isolation and preoccupation awed His disciples who followed
Him. Even at a distance, they were conscious of an atmo-

sphere charged with tremendous happening, and they were apprehensive of what it might involve for themselves (**10**.32).

When He had rejoined them, the Master disclosed in considerable detail what was to happen to Him at Jerusalem at the hands, first, of the priests and scribes, and then, of the Roman judge and his soldiers (33). But he raised the curtain on the ultimate outcome to the extent of announcing His resurrection on the third day (34).

The approach of the two brothers, James and John, seems so out of tune with the spirit of the hour! Sensing, perhaps, that the mission of their Master was now to attain its triumph, they sought a place of eminence in the Messianic Kingdom about to be established. Many of us, if we knew ourselves, would need to admit that we might well have done the same. This had the result of bringing from the Master a response that directed attention to His death as a cup He had to drink, and a baptism in which He was to be immersed (38). Of that cup and baptism they were unfit to partake in the fullest sense at present. Later, however, they would enter into the fellowship of His sufferings as they witnessed for Him.

Christ used the whole untoward incident on the part of the two brothers as an incitement to service, and for an unfolding of the law of precedence in His Kingdom (42 f.). In this He presented Himself as the Great Pattern, and reinforced it by a truly remarkable summing up of His divine mission: 'For the Son of Man also came not to be served, but to serve, and to give His life as a ransom for many' (45). Ransom, denoting payment of a price to secure freedom from captivity, from slavery and from death itself (Exod. **21**.28–30), was integral to the Old Testament idea of redemption. At this hour it would seem, Christ's mind was already travelling through the Old Testament presentation of the Messianic redemption and finding Himself at its heart and centre. He had already before His mind 'the many' whose lives were under forfeit and who should find deliverance through the ransom price that He was to pay, even His own life. Dr. Denney suggests that here 'our Lord condenses in a single phrase the last meaning of His life and death' (*The Death of Christ*, p. 34). Certainly, this 'ransom view' of Christ's life and death has been seen by His Church as unfolding the price of our redemption (1 Cor. **6**.20). This is the only interpretation that satisfies mind and heart, that the life of Christ in its obedience unto death, whatever mystery shrouds it, was placed on the altar as a ransom, the one for the many. Incidentally, 'the many' is probably an echo of Isa. **53**.11 f.

Luke (**12**.50) records a further reference by Christ to His death as a baptism into which He was voluntarily to be plunged. The occasion was His reference to the 'fire' He was to introduce—an experience of suffering in which all His faithful followers were to be involved. But for Himself that fire was already kindled in the enmity and persecution of the Jewish rulers. Far from deflecting Him from His purpose, He was 'constrained' to reach the goal of His earthly life. This word gives expression to the intensity of longing that was almost a pain to Him as it urged Him forward to the appointed end.

It thus became abundantly clear that death was, in Christ's mind, the consummation of His life, the goal to which He was straining with intense desire.

45 : The Attractive Power of the Cross

John 12.20–36

Interesting as it is to find some Greeks—probably Jewish proselytes now attending the Feast at Jerusalem—seeking an interview with Jesus, it is even more interesting to discover His apparent response. Though the motives of the Greek enquirers were beyond suspicion, there is no evidence at all that Jesus granted the interview. Instead, He began to talk darkly of a corn of wheat falling into the ground and dying, and out of its death yielding an abundant harvest. This would seem to imply that the harvest of the Gentile world must await His death. If the request of the Greeks is to suggest an easier way, Jesus dismisses it at once. He announces once again the law of the spiritual Kingdom, which applies to Himself and to all who follow Him, that only in self-giving shall there be self-realization and fulfilment.

To His death Christ here would seem to adopt two differing attitudes. On the one hand, it is to be the hour of the manifestation of His glory (23), on the other, His soul is so troubled at the prospect that he prays to be saved from it (27)—unless the second quotation mark of the RSV (contrast AV) is to be accepted. Yet this shrinking fear, indicating that Jesus was human, yielded immediately to willing submission to a purpose that antedates, and yet controls, all that is happening. Without death that purpose could not be fulfilled.

It is probable that v. 23 is in reality Christ's answer to the request of the Greeks. It is as much as to say: 'The Gentile world must wait the appointed day when the gospel of the Cross shall be preached to the world in the power of the Holy Spirit (Acts 8.4). When that happens the Cross will become the magnet that draws all men to me'. And the events that followed Pentecost proved that only the death of a now living Christ could present the world with the pardon, peace and power that all classes of men need. His hearers found this intimation of His death bewildering. He warned them, however, to accept the light He had brought and to walk in its illumination, since His opportunity for direct speaking with them was now coming to an end.

Again, we repeat, it is now clear that Christ saw quite plainly, and in detail, the way to the Cross that had been appointed Him for the salvation of men, and for overcoming the forces of evil in the world.

46 : The Last Passover and the First Supper

Luke 22.1–23

It was the Passover season. The Jewish rulers were anxious that the teaching of Jesus should not spread further among the multitudes that thronged the city for the Feast. They had to mature their plans quickly and get Jesus out of the way. Judas was the answer to their problem. Under the urge of the evil spirit that took possession of him, he bargained for a private betrayal of his Master that would not precipitate a tumult.

Christ showed how completely He was in control of the situation. He had the place of the Passover fixed and knew He would be welcomed. Seated with the Twelve at the table He expressed His deep desire to eat this particular Passover with them (15). There may have been several reasons for this. The simplest is that He desired their fellowship with Him in His sorrow. He desired also, no doubt, to unveil to them the inner meaning of what was to happen to Him, and so give them this preparation for the ordeal through which they too would have to pass. We now realize that He was establishing this spiritual link between His disciples and their absent Master that would continue until He returned.

When Christ proclaimed that He would not eat 'until it is fulfilled in the kingdom of God' He was probably referring to the events of the next few days, when all that the Passover stood for would receive fulfilment in the divine realm in which it had its source as well as its fulfilment. It is significant how, at a certain stage, Christ seemed to have put the Passover lamb aside and, so to speak, put Himself in its place on the table, saying: 'This is my body . . .' (19). And there the Passover Feast of the Jewish Church merged into the Lord's Supper of the Christian Church.

The Passover was traditionally eaten with bitter herbs, and at the table Christ introduced a detail that was sore to Him and perplexing to them; it was that one of them would betray Him (21). So unsure were they of themselves, that they began to question who of them should do the deed (23, cf. Matt. 26.22).

In the institution of the Lord's Supper the Church turned from the past to find its hope and consolation in the future. And yet at the heart of it all was a body broken and blood shed, which He had turned into a Supper for those that follow Him, a Supper that was and is a fitting prelude to a new morning.

47 : From the Upper Room to the Garden

Luke 22.24–53

The table talk of the disciples was on a lower level than we would expect for the occasion. Sensing that great happenings were about to take place and, perhaps, the kingdom of their dreams about to emerge, they yielded to the old hankering for personal precedence in the new order. To meet the situation Christ reiterated once more the principle of true service, that of humility, and of willingness to be of service to others as the chief honour.

The personal address to Peter was as alarming as it was depressing. Sifting—the separating of grain and chaff—is often given a moral application in Scripture as separating good and evil. As applied to human character it generally stood for the elimination of evil (cf. Christ as winnower in Matt. 3.12). In this case the devil's intention was malevolent and his sifting denoted the destruction of good and the dominance of evil. For that reason, chaff (the mere husk of the grain which in Matt. 3.12 Christ was to burn with 'unquenchable fire') is synonymous with what was worthless and mere sham. It is clear that this was the intention of the devil's sifting of Peter, to leave behind only the chaff, the mere husk of his religion. Christ saw the danger approaching. He had already prayed for them all, but Peter as leading spokesman for the Twelve was the special target. For that reason Christ had specially prayed for him (32) and, though his fall was disclosed, his restoration was assured and a duty assigned him that his sore experience would equip him to render tenderly and compassionately—that of strengthening his brethren. The Master then forewarned them all of the ordeal ahead of them. They would see Him tied, condemned, and crucified, but He assured them that this was happening in fulfilment of prophecy concerning Him (37, cf. Isa. 53.12). Nothing that was to happen to Him was without predetermined spiritual significance (37).

The Garden scene is perhaps the most poignant and heart-moving in all the literature of human suffering. That three chosen disciples should be entrusted to keep watch with Him revealed His sense of weakness and loneliness (40, cf. Matt. 26.37). And yet so great was the pressure of the hour that He put Himself 'a stone's throw' from them as He went forward into the deep shadow of the olive trees. There He saw before Him in vision the cup of suffering that He was to drink on the Cross, and He shrank back in conclusive fear (cf. Mark 14.33 where 'greatly distressed' has the sense of agitation at the sudden appearance of some frightening object). The elements of fear we dimly recognize. In His nature He was perfectly human, and exquisitely sensitive to pain as a sinless human being. In His character He was holy and yet, for our sake, He was to be treated as if He was a sinner. In

71

spirit He was a loving Son, and He was now to meet His Father's frown. But though He prayed that the cup might pass from Him, He acquiesced immediately in what He recognized as His Father's will.

It was at this stage in the agonizing experience of the lonely Sufferer that a message came from Home, 'an angel from heaven', assuring Him, no doubt, that the resources of Heaven were behind Him in the conflict (43). How strength was imparted to Him we cannot know, but it is significant that it was *after* the strengthening that the tension increased and 'his sweat became like great drops of blood' (44).

Note that what was meant to be an 'arrest' was in reality a voluntary surrender (52 ff.). Again, we recognize that He was in control of all the events, and knew that there was an 'hour' given to His enemies to discharge their functions under the powers of darkness.

48 : The Crucifixion

Matthew 27.32–54; John 19.28–30

It is a remarkable feature of the records of the four Gospels that the narrative becomes fuller and more detailed as it approaches the climax of Christ's death. Matthew, Mark and Luke give one-third of their space to 'Holy Week' and John still more. The crucifixion itself is given with great minuteness of detail. This is a clue to the Bible's conception of values.

The site, here called Golgotha, is elsewhere named Calvary. Its precise location is not known for certain. While the suffering involved in crucifixion must have been intense, it is significant that Christ refused to drink the wine mingled with myrrh which was meant to serve as a mild anaesthetic. Apparently He must go through it all in full possession of His feelings and faculties. It is also highly significant that He was placed between two criminals. It was His destiny as Sin-bearer to be 'numbered with the transgressors' (Isa. **53**.12), and as He lived all His life, not as a hermit, but among His fellow men, so He was in death. The inscription written for the Cross by Pilate was worded to offend Jewish religious pride and pour contempt on their political ambitions. It was, in fact, the first line of the New Testament to be committed to writing, and we gather that for one of the two thieves it was the whole Bible, shedding light on the Person and coming glory of the Sufferer in the midst (cf. Luke 23.42).

Matthew gives prominence to the fact that 'from the sixth hour there was darkness over the land until the ninth hour' (45). Was it Nature's expression of sympathy with her suffering Creator? Or did it express the impenetrable agony into which the Sin-bearer was plunged? It was consonant with this outer darkness that the piercing cry should be wrung from the lips of the Sufferer: 'My God, my God, why hast thou forsaken me?' This was no illusion, no collapse of faith, but an experience in which the Sin-bearer was made to feel His position before God. Man had receded from the scene, the transaction was now in the hands of the Supreme Judge of all. But God had not left the scene, even if His favour was temporarily withdrawn, for at that very hour 'God was in Christ reconciling the world to himself' (2 Cor. 5.19).

John records the only cry of physical distress from the lips of Jesus: 'I thirst' (19.28). The vinegar or sour wine offered Him was the Roman soldier's common drink. The offering of it would appear to be the only streak of human kindness in the ghastly scene. As He received it, He rallied His strength to utter the shout of triumph: 'It is finished' (30). Matthew records that He cried 'with a loud voice', as something quite out of the ordinary for a dying man to do (50). It suggests that His life did not ebb out as with ordinary men overtaken by death (cf. Mark 15.44). Rather, in full possession of His strength, He offered Himself, the last sacrifice, of the last priest, on the last altar.

As we leave the scene, we do not know what to wonder at the most, the sin that wrought it and needed it; or the grace and patience that accepted it and endured it; or the love that offered it and executed it!

Of one thing we are sure:

'None of the ransomed ever knew
    How deep were the waters crossed,
Nor how dark was the night that the Lord pass'd through
    Ere He found His sheep that was lost.'

Questions and themes for study and discussion on Studies 41–48

1. To what extent did the 'new wine' of Christ's teaching break through the old wine-skins of traditional Judaism (Luke 5.36–39)? Give some examples.

2. Is it consistent with the deity of Christ that He should feel loneliness, weakness and fear (cf. Heb. 5.7)?

3. What does the introduction: 'The Teacher says' tell about the householder (Luke 22.11)? Would that be adequate to command your obedience?

4. Why do you think Christ prayed, not that Peter might escape the sifting, or that he might not yield to its damaging effects, but rather that his faith in his Master might not be severed?

5. Do you not think it remarkable that Christ actually died by crucifixion, and not by stoning, which was the Jewish form of execution for blasphemy with which Christ was charged (Matt. 26.65)?

   Consider that if it had happened some 40 years earlier, when the Jews were in full authority, would He not have been stoned? Or if it had been 40 years later would He have been crucified at all, since the Romans, then in full power, would not have carried out the sentence of a Jewish court?

   What bearing has this on John's interpretation (19.36 f.)?

   What light does it shed on the Christian interpretation of history?

CHARACTER STUDIES

49 : The Fishermen

Matthew 4.12–25; Mark 1.14–20

By the sixteenth verse of Mark's first chapter Jesus is on the shore of Galilee. There were ample fishing grounds at the head of the lake, and the men who fished the deep waters were among those influenced by John who had preached his fiery sermons far down the same rift-valley. From the fishermen of Galilee Christ called His first disciples.

It was a prosperous and hard-working group of men. They were not wealthy, but comfortable enough, and above all self-employed and independent, no oppressed and exploited class, servile or bitter over their lot. The choice was deliberate. It would have been easy enough in those days of fierce nationalism and class division to collect a horde of the resentful and dispossessed such as David gathered round him in the Adullam cave. But such men were not the material the Lord sought. Those men were to preach a spiritual gospel, not to spearhead a revolutionary movement—a fact to be borne in mind by groups of exotic Christians today.

'Christ,' wrote George Adam Smith, 'went to a trade which had no private wrongs, and called men, not from their dreams, but from work they were contented to do from day to day till something higher should touch them. And so it has come to pass that, not the jargon of the fanatics and brigands of the highlands of Galilee, but the speech of the fishermen of the lake, and the instruments of their simple craft, have become the language and symbolism of Christianity.'

'. . . fishers of men.' It is a vivid image. Peter and Andrew knew the silver heap which turned and tumbled in the straining net as the boats drew them heavily toward the steep beach. They also knew the empty haul, and the whole wet night's labour wasted in unrewarded toil. They knew the bream coming up one by one on the handline—the bream which carried its young in its capacious mouth, and, when

75

they left, adjusted a temporary imbalance with a pebble—or perhaps a lost coin. They understood the figure of speech. We shall meet them again at their higher fishing.

50 : Men of Nazareth

Luke 4.16–30; Mark 6.1–13

The Lord appears to have visited Nazareth, His own home town, twice after the beginning of His public ministry. Luke tells of the first occasion and of the reading from Isaiah, with the significant break after the words 'the acceptable year of the Lord' (cf. Isa. 61.1 f.). The audience listened attentively and were moved by the power of His words, until someone recalled His origin. The remark: 'Is not this Joseph's son?' seems to have provoked a change of mood in the audience and a spirit of hostility which the Lord rebuked in firm terms (23–27). In a concerted demonstration of protest, the congregation arose, and thrust Him before them to the edge of the bluff which overlooks the Esdraelon Plain, perhaps the very place from which, as a boy, He had watched the historic landscape.

At this point, a strange thing happened—'passing through the midst of them he went away.' John also mentions two such incidents. In one of them (10.39) 'they sought again to take Him: and He went forth out of their hand' (RV). The escape in each case was probably due to the Lord's perfect dignity and matchless self-control. Crowds are cowardly. The steady eye, and the level voice of a brave man can often quell a multitude. It will be remembered that officers on one occasion were sent to arrest the Lord. They came back to their masters without carrying out their orders. 'Why did you not bring him?' say the irate priests. 'No man ever spoke like this man,' answer the men (John 7.45 f.). It was their only excuse! Imagine a police officer giving as a reason for not carrying out an order, the dominating personality of the man he was sent to take . . . And imagine his excuse being accepted! Yet, this is what happened. The Pharisees knew that there was a spell and a power in the words of Christ, which struck awe into those that heard them. They knew it from experience. So with the crowd. As the Lord

76

moved through them they fell back. Their arms were power-less to strike Him. A glance, and they quailed.

So too in Mark's story, if he is describing another occa-sion. It was the fact that they knew Him that blocked their capacity for belief, and without their belief, the One who sought to bless them was powerless to act (6.5). Poor men of Nazareth—so needy, so sceptical, and, in consequence, so deprived.

51 : Men of Capernaum

Mark 1.21–2.12; Luke 4.31–44

The people of Nazareth rejected their townsman on the absurd grounds that they knew Him. He was only the local carpenter's son. Therefore He could have no message for them. Capernaum was across the length of Galilee, near the head of the lake—no great distance as today counts distance, but far enough for those who trod the long, rough roads. Capernaum scatters its ruins today on a deserted shore, but in the Lord's day the traffic of a great east-west road passed through the town, and the industry of the lake had one of its centres there.

The people of Capernaum caught the note of authority in His voice, and the population found Him speaking to their hearts. He was never again to be so accepted. We catch glimpses of the men and women who found blessing there, and shall meet more as the story proceeds; Peter's wife's mother, the tormented and deranged, and the paralysed man who had four good friends (Mark 2.3) . . .

The story is told in the Second Gospel with peculiar vividness. Mark was Peter's pupil. Mark, counselled and healed by Peter after his wounding failure on the missionary journey with Paul, had been set to work on his real task by the great apostle who had probably led him to Christ as a boy. The story of Christ which he wrote, the earliest of the four, was at Peter's suggestion, and from Peter's informa-tion. Again and again, it almost seems that we can hear Peter's voice behind the brief chapters.

In the story of the man with the four good friends we sense strongly Peter's interest. Was Peter one of the four?

Was it Peter's house, the tiling of which was removed to secure access? Were the ropes for the delicate operation secured from Peter's boat, moored, perhaps, within running distance? Was it Peter who was determined that the crowd, composes it appears, of Pharisaic critics, should not stand in the way of blessing for a needy friend? We can never know, but the picture emerges of the common people of the lakeside town, recognizing the day of their visitation, and, unlike the men of Nazareth, conscious of the power, the authority and the worth of the One who came among them. Authority—how the world yearns for it in the Christian message! How helpless is the man who faces the world without it!

52 : The Pharisees

Mark 2.23–3.30

Observing the Lord's popularity among the common people who 'heard him gladly' (Mark 12.37), the Pharisees of Capernaum went to work. They invited some of the leading members of their sect down from Jerusalem to assess the situation. The pundits came, considered the case, and delivered their verdict: 'He casts out devils by the prince of devils.' In a few words the Lord demolished the absurd statement, but He continued with a statement of terrible seriousness. Here it is in Edward Vernon's little-known paraphrase of Mark's Gospel: 'But now let me tell you very solemnly: People will be forgiven all kinds of wickedness, even the vilest sins and the unholiest talk, but to call the goodness of God the work of the devil, and to call God's Spirit an evil spirit, is a sin past forgiving.'

Who were the people to whom these terribly serious words were addressed? We have seen in an earlier volume how exile turned the Hebrew captives back to their Scriptures. The Pharisees (and the name appears to mean 'the Separated'), were the leaders in this biblical revival. The Law was their incessant study. We have seen how the stress of exile divided the Jews. Some like Daniel, stood firm. Some like Esther and Mordecai conformed. From the Daniels came the Pharisees.

In ardour, faith and dedication they did fine work. And then, like so many who thus begin, they ended in pride and pettiness, 'separated' not from paganism, evil and compromise, but from the mass of Israel, the 'accursed crowd' (John 7.49). The Law became, not a means to holiness, but holiness itself, a clutter of man-made regulations which they themselves could only keep by inventing, along with their detailed obligations, a parallel series of escape clauses, which poisoned their practice with hypocrisy.

They were not all corrupted in this manner. We shall meet Nicodemus. We shall meet Gamaliel. But such was the degeneration of a once noble order, that the Pharisee was capable of the sombre sin of Capernaum; the blindness, blasphemy and stark evil which could attribute the visible works of God in human lives to the power of evil. Such is sin unpardonable, for none could so calmly speak unless mind and heart were hardened and calloused beyond all possibility of repentance. We must pause in the next study to look more closely at this situation.

53 : The Doomed

Matthew 12.22 50; Luke 11.14 20; 1 Corinthians 6.9–11

No mortal man can pronounce another living person finally doomed. Christ alone of those who have walked the earth had the right to do so. He told the proud Pharisees that they had sinned beyond forgiveness. Thus came into the New Testament 'the unpardonable sin'.

Who are the doomed? Not those who have committed any of the common sins which damage, mar and ruin human life. The list of those who have thus sinned and been forgiven is evidence enough. Jacob was a liar, a cheat, deceiver of his old father, greedy, treacherous. In fierce conflict he found peace with God. In an earlier study we have lingered with David, the murderer and adulterer, who wrote Psalm 51. We shall meet Matthew and Zacchaeus, cynical collaborators for gain with those who trod down their countrymen. One of them wrote a book of the New Testament. The Prodigal Son of the famous story wasted a fortune in carnal sin. He was weak, selfish and unloving. His father received him, and killed the fattened calf. The bandit on the cross was a man of blood and violence. Christ accepted him. Peter denied his Lord and was recommissioned. Paul was the rabid persecutor of Christian men and women. He acquiesced in Stephen's death. He became the great apostle to the Gentiles.

And look at the list of sinners in the letter to Corinth. They were all forgiven. What did Christ say? 'Him who comes to me, I will not cast out.' Both of the available Greek negatives are used in the verse. It is impossible to make a more emphatic negative assertion. 'If anyone, anyone at all, at an·· time, with any past, from any sin, comes in penitence ۔o me, I will not under any conceivable circumstances turn that person away.' Can a promise be more absolute? Could it have been made by One more utterly true?

We have lingered a little on this theme because it can stir unhealthy fear. In the hundreds of characters of the Bible at which we have looked over these two years or more, we have met all kinds of sinners, and we have seen them again and again forgiven. Who then are the doomed? We shall look further tomorrow.

54 : The Doomed Again

Isaiah 1.1–18; Revelation 22.1–12

We have seen that all sins brought into the presence of God can find forgiveness. God remembers them no more. 'Though your sins be like scarlet,' runs a verse in the first chapter of Isaiah, 'they shall be white as snow.' And Isaiah had in mind the deep scarlet, shot with purple, which the Phoenicians made from the juice of the murex shellfish of the Palestine coast, a colour which impregnated the tissues of the garment beyond all possibility of washing away. God forgives, and will always forgive, when sin is brought to Him in confession.

What then of these men to whom Christ addressed His terrible words? Consider the subject thus: God's Spirit prompts men to face the challenge of Christ. When awareness of his passenger broke upon Peter in his fisher's boat, he cried: 'Depart from me, for I am a sinful man, O Lord.' They were wild, impulsive words, typical of Peter. Christ does not abandon those who thus respond. He draws near to save. To face Christ's challenge is overwhelming—but salvation.

But consider the contrary reaction. Dogged refusal to respond to the promptings of God's Spirit, in pride of heart or deliberately cherished hatred, diminishes the ability of heart and mind to grasp the idea of truth, goodness and beauty. Continue such determined wickedness long enough, and a spiritual paralysis envelops the personality. It is a self-willed hardness, not a statement couched in words, which constitutes 'blasphemy' of the sort Christ described.

The Pharisees in Capernaum had declared, as we have seen, in measured and deliberate terms, that Christ's work was evil work; He used Satanic power to bring peace to tormented lives. Thus to pervert truth and spurn goodness, was to demonstrate evil so determined and ingrained, a spirit so past all response to grace, a conscience so crushed and seared and a heart so wilfully hardened, that Christ (and only Christ could so diagnose) could declare that such men were already past the possibility of claiming God's forgiveness. Like the wicked friar, pictured by Dante in his *Inferno*, they were men with souls already in Hell while their bodies lived on earth. Such are the doomed—characters whom God alone can name.

And it follows that no one need fear 'the unpardonable sin'. The viciously impenitent care nothing for it. Mr. Fearing spoils life, and jettisons the joy and peace of mind which he was meant to enjoy. But he is received at last. No penitent was ever rejected for 'the unpardonable sin', for its very mark is impenitence.

55 : The Mason

Mark 3.1–12; Luke 4.38–44

The crowded weeks in and around Capernaum left a mass of stories which found their way into the accounts of all the evangelists. The man in the synagogue with the withered hand has a place in three of them, probably because of his healing evoked the bitter response of the Pharisees, and the beginnings of that campaign of hate which was to end at Calvary, and justify the Lord's denunciation of their wickedness.

But the man, like the mother of Peter's wife, restored by

Christ to usefulness and service, is worth looking at for his own sake. There is a legend which could be true, that the man approached Christ with the moving and simple words: 'I was a mason, winning my livelihood with my hands. I beg you, restore me to soundness, that I may not have the shame of begging for my food.'

According to the clutter of laws with which the Pharisees had loaded the observation of the Sabbath, only when life was endangered, could healing be permitted on the seventh day. The Lord brought the man forward. 'Is it lawful on the sabbath to do good or to do harm?' He asked 'to save life or to kill?' It was a skilful question, for the rabbis had decreed that if a beast had fallen into a pit on the Sabbath, the owner was to ascertain whether it was hurt. If not, he was to feed and bed it, but not extricate it until the next day. If it was hurt, he was to get it out and kill it. This was difficult and wasteful, so they had an escape regulation. The owner could get the beast out of the pit with the announced intention of killing it, and then not do so. In other words, they could twist their own laws for an animal but not for a man.

So was a man's usefulness restored. No doubt he went back to his mallet and chisel, as Peter's wife's mother rose from her bed and resumed her household tasks. Christ's presence in the life is a force which sanctifies, but also restores a man to normality and usefulness. His benediction takes away the spoiling, paralysing maladies which destroy calm and strength. To begin the life-long task of becoming like Him, is to begin moving towards the personality God intended us to be.

As with the mason of Capernaum, so with those who at His command stretch forth the hand today in another world, another century—

> *But this I know, He heals the brokenhearted,*
> *And stays our sin, and calms our lurking fear,*
> *And lifts the burden from the heavy laden,*
> *For yet the Saviour, Saviour of the world, is here.*

Questions and themes for study and discussion on Studies 49–55

1. The place of natural ability and self-sacrifice in Christian service.
2. Why is it impossible for Christ to act in a climate of unbelief?
3. Signs of Peter's reporting in the narrative of Mark.
4. 'Conviction of sin'—when is it healthy and when morbid?
5. On what is God's forgiveness based?
6. What is a 'seared conscience'? What leads to it?
7. How can faith calm fear?

THE WORK OF CHRIST

The Teaching of Peter

As already indicated, it was obviously in the mind of Christ to commit the full revelation and interpretation of His saving work to His apostles. We can claim, indeed, that it is their doctrine that most adequately explains the gospel facts. The Gospel narratives of the life and death of Jesus remain obscure and, to a large extent, lacking in purpose, without the apostolic doctrine to interpret and elucidate them. Peter's intimacy with the Lord in His earthly life and his call to apostleship qualify him outstandingly for this task and claim for him a special hearing when he seeks to evaluate the facts.

56 : Fulfilment and Promise

Acts 3.13–26

The familiar sight of a cripple sitting at the Gate Beautiful of the Temple seeking alms, presented a challenge to the new Faith, and to the experience of Pentecost that the disciples had just been through. This challenge of the commonplace became very real, and it could not be ignored. The miracle of healing took place, and it posed a question as to the source of the power that put the crippled man on the road again. Peter seizes the occasion to proclaim the power of the ascended and glorified Lord as that which restored the man to health.

Peter is careful, however, to connect all that had happened in the past few weeks with the promises of God given through the prophets down the ages. But the fact that God's purpose lay behind it did not exonerate the Jews from the guilt of the crucifixion, and Peter's vivid words pressed home the magnitude of the crime (15). It was not the Cross in isolation that Peter interpreted; it was the Cross as seen in the light of the ascension and glorification of Jesus, which had placed the divine seal on what had happened at Calvary.

The *name*, or authority, of that glorified Lord was the source of the power into which they were inquiring.

Basing it on the reality of Christ's death and resurrection, Peter presented to the Jews the call to repentance and a renunciation of the sins of the past (19). Their conversion would not only result in the personal experience of forgiveness, but in hastening the times of blessing that God had promised as the distinctive feature of the new era (19), and so usher in the personal return of the Lord Jesus Christ (20).

The main emphasis of Peter's message was that the present was rooted in the past, and would reach its complete fulfilment in the future. The Messianic promises regarding the Servant of the Lord (13) had, up to that point, found fulfilment in the sufferings of Jesus of Nazareth, and would find complete fulfilment in the age to come. Peter thus placed the Cross at the heart and centre of world history.

57 : Preaching the Cross

Acts 4.23–31; 5.27–32

It is significant that when the Christians thanked God for rescuing Peter and John from the Jewish rulers, it was done in the words of the Old Testament Scriptures (Psa. 2), with which they were familiar. The application of the words to Jesus, especially to the circumstances of the crucifixion, was a transition very easily made. It is a sobering thought to us still that Jew and Gentile, Herod and Pilate, the priests and the Roman soldiers, representing religion at its purest and civil justice at its highest, were partners in the act and share responsibility for the crime. Note the futility of Pilate's spectacular hand-washing (Matt. 27.24).

Behind the jealousy of the Jewish rulers and the injustice of the Roman Judge, the disciples could discern the wider pattern that revealed the hand and purpose of God (4.28). The burden of their prayer was, not their own safety, but the opportunity to witness to their Lord and to have that witness sealed by the power of God (29 f.). And they received an immediate answer in a manifestation of God's power that was reminiscent of Pentecost, resulting in a fresh filling of the Spirit (31).

The disciples used the miraculous deliverance of their leaders to preach the gospel still more openly, Peter being their spokesman (5.29). Their chief offence, as it appeared to the Council, was 'to teach in this name' (28). Note the reluctance even to mention the now hateful name of Jesus. Peter did not hesitate to reiterate their guilt in the crucifixion of One who was demonstrably the Messiah of Israel (31). The resurrection and exaltation only served to confirm His Messiahship, but He now uses His exalted position as 'Leader and Saviour' to give to Israel the opportunity for repentance and forgiveness of sins (31). This testimony to what Christ is and does, combining power and grace, shows how He continues to be involved in the work of salvation.

Note that the apostles did not consider the work of Christ as finished with His death. In the practical sense, we may almost say that it began with His resurrection and exaltation, in the power of which He grants the forgiveness of sins as the supreme gift of His death. Never forget that Jesus Christ is alive!

58 : The Precious Blood of Christ

1 Peter 1.1, 2, 10–21

We have an opportunity here to discover, not only what Peter himself thought of the death of Christ, but what His death was meaning to 'exiles of the Dispersion,' some of them being Jews living outside Palestine, and many belonging to the slave population who had no country they could call their own. What Peter had to say to them derived additional weight from the fact that he was 'a witness of the sufferings of Christ' (5.1).

Peter reminds his readers of their privileges as Christians. Basic to all was their election in the eternal covenant. The purpose of that election is well translated by the TEV: 'to be made a holy people (set apart for God) by His Spirit, and to obey Jesus Christ and be made clean by his blood' (2).

Later in this chapter Peter links us once again with the Old Testament expectations of the Messiah (10). The prophets looked forward to the day when the promises they were inspired to give would receive fulfilment, and they searched their own Scriptures to find this out. These promises specially concerned the suffering Saviour and the glory that would result from His sufferings. Into all this the unfallen angels, Peter says, desired to gaze, no doubt as a further unveiling of the glory of their God.

The practical significance of the sufferings of Christ for those scattered Christians was that these sufferings urged them to a life of holiness. The death of Christ established new relations to a holy God, who required from them a holiness that had its inspiration and pattern in His own holiness (15 f.). Christ's death (His 'blood') made this holiness possible for them.

Note the price of redemption. It was 'the precious blood of Christ'. Silver and gold were given for the manumission of slaves, but it represented a 'perishable' standard of values. The blood of Christ was precious in the sense that in the eternal scale of values it was for ever competent. For that reason their ransom price could never be challenged, nor their security disturbed.

Redemption in Christ brought entirely new values into the personal life of the Christian who sought holiness of character, values that took no stock of the foolish and futile religious customs of the past (18). Note that redemption by blood is here traced back to the Old Testament revelation, and still further back to the purpose of God 'before the foundation of the world' (20).

Does your redemption mean more, or less to you because you can trace it back to an eternal purpose of love?

59 : Christ Brings us to God

1 Peter 2.18–25; 3.13–4.2

In the first of these passages Peter had in view the obedience that slaves were required to give to their masters. It often involved suffering, and suffering unjustly, but he elevates such suffering into a divine calling (21), as he finds in it an analogy to the sufferings of Jesus Christ, their Example in character, as in all life.

Christ's sufferings had, however, this unique quality, that they were *wholly* unmerited. His conduct under suffering was a submission and self-denial that did not even plead for His rights (22 f.). Though He had been suffering all His life from the unkindness and malice of His fellow men, these sufferings reached their consummation and climax on the Cross.

But Christ in His sufferings is more than Example. He is Redeemer. It was 'our sins' He bore (24)—Peter here placed himself alongside the Christian slaves he was addressing. Bearing 'our sins' was a relationship with us which caused Christ intense personal suffering. In all the deep sensitivity of His humanity—all the more sensitive because He 'committed no sin' of His own (22)—He 'bore' our sins, accepted the relationship they involved towards God and so their consequences, in a way we cannot understand. Christ experienced the full implications of this situation 'on the tree', or 'right up to the tree', the place of utmost sin-bearing.

For those who are identified with Christ by faith, this sin-bearing means both death and life. It means death to the old life of sin, and life in a new sphere, that of righteousness as the ruling principle of the new life. Thus it is that by His 'wounds', or bruises—and the slave-class knew what that meant—healing came to them, even when they were suffering unjustly.

In the second passage (3.13–4.2) Peter reverts to the sufferings of the slave-class among his readers. When they were suffering for their convictions they could look to Christ their Lord, who suffered as the Righteous for the unrighteous. But again, He is not the mere Example. He is the Restorer. He suffered to bring us to God; to remove our estrangement, open for us a way of access, and bring us there in an experience of pardon and peace. In dying as the Righteous One, who took over the accountability of unrighteous ones, He died death outright, as every other human being dies. This, in fact, is what is meant by His 'descent into Hades' (as the Apostles' Creed puts it), entering the realm of the dead. But He was quickened and raised from the dead by the Spirit. What is meant by Christ preaching to the 'spirits in prison' is not known to us with any degree of certainty, and does not belong, in any way we can understand, to His redeeming work (19).

The passage ends on the note of absolute and complete victory for the suffering Servant (22), the note on which Isa.

53, to which it bears such close resemblance in its language, also closes.

Questions and themes for study and discussion on Studies 56–59

1. Consider the extent to which the incident of the crippled man sitting at the Gate Beautiful of the Temple illustrates:

   (a) The impotence of a merely ritualistic religion

   (b) The power of a living faith.

2. What light does it cast on the world order that religion at its purest, represented by the Jews, and civil justice at its highest, represented by the Romans, combined to crucify Jesus?

3. 'Crucified and killed by the hands of lawless men' (Acts 2.23); 'Delivered up according to the definite plan and foreknowledge of God' (Acts 2.23); 'No one takes it (life) from me . . . I have power to lay it down, and I have power to take it up again' (John 10.18). How would you reconcile these three statements?

4. How does Christ in His death 'bring' us to God, and to what kind of God does He restore us?

CHARACTER STUDIES

60 : The Tax Collectors

Matthew 11.20–30; Mark 2.13–20; Luke 5.27–32

Our readings must sometimes be repetitive because it is difficult in the tumult of events recorded in the narratives of the
Galilean mission to disentangle character from character,
and event from event. We have seen the Lord turning from
those whom He ironically described as 'righteous', to the
common people and the needy.

The conversion of one Levi, the Matthew of the First
Gospel, led to a contact with a despised and hated group of
men, the 'publicani' or tax-gatherers, so lamentably rendered
'publicans' in the AV (KJV). Who were these men? It was
common Roman practice to farm out the taxes of a province. Financial organizations would bid a fixed sum and
were free to recoup themselves. These were the men who
were in direct contact with the people, and who, each in his
petty sphere, reflected the rapacity, the corruption and the
cruelty to which the whole vicious system lent itself.

All over the Empire men cried out in protest against the
tax collectors. A grim anthology of scorn and hatred can be
gathered from surviving literature against them. They were
'licensed thieves', 'wild beasts in the shape of men' . . . 'The
tax-man gave a present to the merchant! After this will not
wolves drop lambs from their teeth and lions let fawns go
free?'

In no place was such anger so hot as in Palestine, where
all tribute was looked upon as a symbol of subjection.
Patriotism and religion combined in resistance to the system,
and it followed that no man would undertake the task of
gathering the tribute unless he was cynically prepared to set
religion, patriotism and the regard of his fellows all second
to gain. The tax-man was the pariah of society, loathed,
scorned, rejected. He could not serve as a witness in a Jewish
court. He was excluded from all religious worship.

Set as it was on a great commercial highway, Capernaum

had a large group of tax collectors, who, as the victims of a common hatred, formed their own social group. Matthew was one of them. Excluded from the synagogue, he must have heard the Lord preach on shore or field, and found his heart moved to yearning for a better life. Such desire does not go unnoticed by God. Matthew left his office and followed Christ.

61 : Matthew

Hosea 6.1–6; Acts 1.1–8; Matthew 8.19–22

Look again at the thrice-told story of the call of Levi, who was to be known as Matthew. He was called directly from his place of business, and followed without hesitation. But he carried over into his new life some of the qualities which he had no doubt exercised in the corrupt businesses of the tax-office. Instinctively Matthew grasped a prime principle of witness. It begins 'at Jerusalem'. And secondly it cuts through all impediments.

The only contact with the world's need was among the outcasts of his own class. That is why, 'in his own house' (Luke 5.29), he made a banquet for the tax officials. He met them where they could be met, and found Christ with him. Mark adds the surprising detail (2.15) that there were 'many who followed him'. The imperfect tense used here might be better rendered 'they were many, and they were for following him.' That is, contrary to all popular expectation, there were many among the despised group who had felt the power of the Lord's words. The world is too often ignorant of the agony of mind and misery which lie behind some hard and seemingly defiant exterior. But the Lord, as John was to remark, 'knew what was in man' (2.25).

There had no doubt been many a wild carousel in that same diningroom, and it was an appropriate place for the renegade son of Levi's tribe to bring together his old companions in sin to hear his farewell to an evil life, and to meet his new Master. There was little privacy in an ancient town. The house, as custom was, stood open, and no one had to peer through curtained windows to see the Lord at table with the hated group. It appears from Matthew (9.10), that the disciples who had already been called, also joined the company, but perhaps with some visible embarassment, or obviously less at ease than their Master.

Hence the direction of the Pharisees' attack. Perhaps they saw an opportunity to drive a wedge between Him and His followers, for it was to the disciples that they made their protest. The Lord heard them and rebuked them. It is touchingly significant that Matthew alone records the sentence from Hosea (6.6; Matt. 9.13): 'It is mercy that I desire and not sacrifice.' Mercy is what Matthew had found,

62 : Matthew the Writer

Jeremiah 33; Zechariah 9.9

We should pause at this point to consider what Matthew did for the Lord he had found, for in the historian we find the man. Old tradition has it that Matthew's first writing was a collection of the sayings of Christ. Perhaps the first impact of the Lord on Matthew's mind was in the authoritative nature of His teaching (7.29), and, being a man who knew professionally the importance of accurate records, he set out to capture on papyrus the precious words he heard.

The collection of sayings which Matthew made no longer exists in such a form, but perhaps we can see the shape of it in the Gospel which ultimately emerged and absorbed the earlier work. The book is dominated by five discourses (chs. 5–7; 10; 13; 18; 23–25), each recording an aspect of the Lord's teaching.

Here was a man captivated by the words of Christ, heard, not in the synagogue where his kind were unwelcome, but from the edge of the crowd, in the street, from the report of others, and perhaps written down immediately to retain them and hold their meaning fast. So perhaps began the task which preserved for the world the Sermon on the Mount.

And then came the incredible moment of the invitation to join the band of those who walked with Him. Matthew followed, counting no cost, and the One whom he had known afar became a close and revered friend, as well as Master and Lord. And in that experience wonder grew. He saw the royalty of Christ, searching out, or perhaps already knew, the kingly oracles of the Old Testament, and found prophecy fulfilled. He chose the Davidic genealogy, and uses frequently the royal title 'the Son of David'. In the Nativity stories he chooses to tell of the august Magi, leaving Luke to tell of the shepherds. Both Matthew and Luke tell of the triumphant procession into Jerusalem but only Matthew quotes the prophecy.

Matthew, too, has more to say than others on 'the Kingdom of God'. He alone records the words about the coming Church, and leads on to the Great Commission to the disciples and the promise of Christ's continuing presence with His own. 'The style is the man', as the saying runs, and if we would know the one time tax collector, we must look rather at the truths and facts which he stressed in writing than in words which he spoke, for they are few.

63 : The Twelve

Matthew 10.1–11.1

We have looked at the fishermen of Galilee, those vigorous and industrious men whom the Lord called to follow Him. They were most probably converts of John the Baptist, their hearts prepared by the desert preacher for the call which was to come. We have met Levi, who was named Matthew, and who was called, not from the fishing-boat, but from the tax-office in the lakeside town.

At some point in the ministry in Galilee the band became complete. The Lord chose twelve, perhaps with the thought in mind of the twelve tribes of Israel. We shall meet many of them again, and have occasion to observe facets of their characters, but we should now look at them together. They were far from being the 'twelve ragamuffins' of King Frederick's letter to Voltaire.

The Twelve were called apostles, and the word implies that they were special messengers, bearing a commission, and, in fulfilling that task, wielding their Master's own authority. First, there was Simon, called Peter, whom we shall meet frequently. Peter and Andrew his brother were fishermen of Bethsaida, and met Jesus early, down at Bethany beyond Jordan. John tells us that these men were disciples of the Baptist.

Andrew had the distinction of being the first missionary of the Church, for he it was who sought Peter and brought him to Christ. Peter was a prize—'the mouth of the apostles', Chrysostom called him. To be sure, there were times when Peter spoke unwisely, but there is no denying his worth and his place in ancient history. David Smith wrote well of him: 'That impulsive man, so prone to err, so quick to repent . . . continually blundering, and in the panic of the last dread crisis guilty of a dire infidelity; nevertheless his very blunders were born of the ardour of his love for Jesus, and in the hour of his unfaithfulness, a look from that dear face broke his heart. When all was over, he could lift his eyes and say: Lord you know all things; you know that I love you.'

Next, another pair of brothers, also disciples of the Baptist, James and John. Their father Zebedee was a prosperous man, and their mother, probably a sister of the Virgin, was an ambitious woman, but brave, for she stood by the cross. It was her ardent spirit which lived in her boys whom Jesus called 'the Sons of Thunder'. James died at the hands of Herod Agrippa. John was to outlive the whole band . . . These men formed an inner circle of the Twelve.

64 : The Twelve Again

John 1.35–51; 1 Corinthians 12.12–31

There are some matters of interest which these studies necessarily bypass. The chronology of the Gospels, the order of recorded events and utterances, is not our immediate interest. We follow roughly the order of the first of the Gospels to be written, that of Mark, and draw into the list of characters studied parallel accounts in the other evangelists. Readers, however, must have observed already in the passages prescribed some divergences of order which call for explanation. Those interested would find Dr. Donald Guthrie's excellent *Shorter Life of Christ* a great help as an ancillary study. The matter is mentioned because the reading for this study raises the question of a period in Judea before the mission in Galilee.

But to continue with the Twelve. Philip was called at this time, a cautious and wary man, who liked demonstrable certainty. There is room for such men in the Church. They are a salutary check on the 'sons of thunder', and even on the

'Peters' of the community. Philip seems to have been a friend of Andrew.

Bartholomew is not mentioned again. It is said that, like Thomas, he ended as a missionary in India, no unlikely tradition, for the Italian shipmen now knew the secret of the alternating monsoons, and regularly traded with India, a fact to which many a hoard of Roman coins bears witness. There is also room in the Church for multitudes who never reach the headlines—nor want to do so. It is possible that Bartholomew was Nathanael, for just as the other evangelists do not mention Nathanael, so John, who does mention him, never mentions Bartholomew. Perhaps the full name was Nathanael Bar Tolmai (that is 'son of Tolmai'). We shall speak of him again.

Next came Thomas and Matthew. We have met Matthew and need say no more of him, but who was Thomas? The word means, like Didymus, its Greek equivalent, 'a twin'. Was he, as Eusebius said, another Judas? He was a devoted man but a confirmed pessimist.

James the son of Alphaeus, nicknamed 'the Little' (which may mean 'the younger') to distinguish him from the son of Zebedee, was, says tradition, a tax collector, converted in Matthew's house. If Alphaeus was also the father of Levi, then James was the brother of Matthew, and if Alphaeus was Clopas, then the Mary, wife of Clopas, who stood by the cross, was the mother of Matthew and James. What a household if these assumptions hold!

65 : The Rest of the Twelve

John 14

There must have been three among the apostles who bore the very common name of Judas. The Judas who is mentioned along with James, son of Alphaeus, is called by Matthew Thaddaeus. If this is from the Aramaic term Taddai it distinguishes him from Judas, called Thomas, the Twin, because Taddai means 'the courageous'. Mark calls him Lebbaeus, and if this is from the Aramaic Libbai, meaning 'the hearty', it distinguishes him from the cold and calculating Judas Iscariot. This faithful Judas appears again only once, in the puzzled remark of John 14.22.

95

And now another Simon, distinguished from Simon Peter by being called the Canaanite or the Zealot. The first term probably means that he came from Cana in Galilee, the second is much more sinister. If Simon was a Zealot, he had been a sworn member of a desperate band of terrorists, who, during the census troubles of A.D. 7, had vowed hostility to Rome. To accept such a man among the apostles, was to court the suspicion of Rome, whose agents and Jewish collaborators were very well informed on all such vital matters of security. The Zealots were diametrically opposed to the other type of Jew, such as Matthew, who took service under the occupying authorities or their Herodian associates. It is a most striking testimony to the unifying power of Christ, that Matthew and Simon could find a comon meeting place in His fellowship.

The last on the list was Judas Iscariot, the future betrayer. The surname probably means that he came from Kerioth in southern Judea. Judas Iscariot seems to have been the only member of the band who was not a native of Galilee. Why Jesus chose him, and why Judas became what he did become, is a problem we shall meet again.

But observe that the apostles were all young men. Peter alone appears to have been married. Jesus Himself seems to have been a father among them (Mark 10.24; John 13.33; 14.18). They were young men, still unfettered by custom, unbound by the prejudice which sometimes comes with years, still sensitive to wonder and unbounded hope. Except perhaps for Nathanael, they were not students, and none of them had the massive learning of Paul, their future associate. This is the band which set out to subdue the world.

66 : Nathanael

John 1.43–51; Genesis 28

Nathanael was a man who required convincing. Philip knew this, and set the phrases of his announcement in careful order. Look again at John 1.45. He mentions Moses first, and the humble Joseph last. It was as Philip must have expected. Nathanael fixed immediately on Nazareth. Not only was the town without clear reference in the Old Testament, it was also the most cosmopolitan place of Galilee, and, though

Galilee was not as Gentile-ridden as the Decapolis, on the other side of the lake, it was full enough of foreigners to call forth the scornful remark of the determined Israelite. A Messiah from Nazareth, indeed!

Then why was Nathanael so rapidly convinced (49)? The answer must lie in the Lord's strange remark in the previous verse (48). Nathanael obviously understood Christ's words more intimately than the rest who heard them. What if his morning meditation in some garden or orchard place of prayer (48, 50) had been the story of Jacob, who, full of guile and double-dealing though he was, saw a vision of great temple-steps leading up to God, and visible communication between God and man? Jacob of all men!

To a man so liable to fail, Nathanael may have mused, God granted a covenant, and a vision of Israel's destiny. But now, for all the prophetic fervour of John's ministry, and the breath of real revival through the land, the heavens seemed closed, and God remote. The covenant appeared forgotten, and God careless of His own. Looking at him, and hinting that He knew mysteriously the subject of Nathanael's complaint, the Lord utters the significant words of v. 47. 'No guile' refers surely to the fault of Jacob. 'Angels ascending and descending' on one who was the true path to God (John 14.6) shows the same covert reference to Genesis 28. This was the secret communication between the Lord and Nathanael.

Hence the sudden fervour of Nathanael's surrender. God had met him in the place of prayer. In Christ Nathanael encountered One who understood his dreams, and satisfied the deeper longings of his heart. In a bent and twisted world, to know God is to know One, at least, who understands.

Questions and themes for study and discussion on Studies 60–66

1. How may the home be used in evangelism?
2. How do Matthew's Nativity stories differ from Luke's?
3. Could you match the apostles with twelve similar characters from your own church?
4. List the faults of the apostles already visible. Do faults preclude usefulness?
5. Why Twelve? Was there any special significance in the number?

THE WORK OF CHRIST

The Teaching of Paul

To Paul the death of Christ was not merely a doctrine; it was a gospel. For him the good news of salvation flows from that source alone, and is applicable to the whole of human personality in all its relationships.

67: The Righteousness of God

Romans 3.19–26; 5.6–11

In his argument, from 1.18 to this point in his letter, Paul brings mankind to the place, morally and spiritually, where all argument in self-defence ceases, and all the world is found guilty before God (19). Furthermore, there is no help for man in any of the expedients of the past. The Old Testament ritual and all its temporary requirements serve only to expose our sin, and cannot remove it (20).

Into that situation Paul introduces a new term—but a favourite one with him—the righteousness of God. This is used in two senses: (a) the righteousness which God demands because it is the expression of His own character, and (b) the righteousness which God provides when, having none of our own, He accepts us in Christ His Son (22). This is indeed the Good News of Paul's gospel, that the righteousness which God demands, God now provides.

The way in which that righteousness—the reality of being right with God—can be made over to us is the discussion in vs. 24 f. There three figures are used (a) that of the law courts, (b) that of the release of slaves, and (c) that of sacrifice. (a) In the presence of God we may be declared just in relation to His demands on us (24a). (b) This is bestowed on us because of the ransom price paid for us and still valid in Christ (24b). (c) Christ in this relation to us is our divinely appointed 'expiation', mercy-seat or 'propitiation' (AV), where faith meets with His shed blood (25). It is because of Christ's death that God is seen to be righteous, when He proclaims as righteous in His sight the one who is united to His Son. Christ's death is also the basis on which God's relationship to His believing people in past ages is seen to be just (25 f.).

In Rom. 5.6–11 we have our redemption in Christ related to our life in its entirety, both now and for ever. This was a stupendous act of divine grace, because it was when we were helpless to mend our relationship with God that Christ died for us, ungodly as we are: There could be no greater manifestation of His love (8). Through Christ's blood we have three blessings: safety from the judgement sin deserves in the day of final reckoning (9); our being sustained by the life of the Christ who reconciled us (10); and joy because of what Christ has done (11).

These two passages probably present, in short compass, the most comprehensive presentation of the work of Christ as reconciling, preserving, and satisfying, that we have in the Bible.

68 : 'The Sweet Exchange'

2 Corinthians 5.11–21

The driving force behind all Paul's activities—misunderstood as they often were—was 'the love of Christ'. This was the personal love that Christ had for him, and the responsive love that it created in his heart. Paul holds that this love must operate in the lives of all who died with Christ, and now live with Him and for Him (15).

It is this love that makes Paul view his fellow men in a new light. He does not regard them simply as men to be judged by their external circumstances, but as men for whom Christ died. In the same way he regards Christ, not as he once judged Him, a mere man, but as the divine Lord (16). This relationship to Christ transforms all His people, creating them as new persons for whom everything has become new. The old opinions, views, desires, ambitions, are gone, and entirely new values, aims and principles, take their place, and have God as their Author.

To His reconciled people God has given a 'message of reconciliation' based on what He has done in His Son Jesus Christ (19). This involves being ambassadors of Christ, pleading with all men in Christ's name to be at peace with God. For God was acting on our behalf in Christ when He identified Him with our sin, though He had no sin of His own, in order that we might be identified with the righteousness of God, though we had no righteousness of our own. So it was not merely the One for the many, but the Righteous for the unrighteous.

Here we are at the heart of Paul's gospel: that Christ took our place in order that we might take His. He became a sin-bearer—not a sinner—in order that we might become bearers of His righteousness. This is what made an Early Father of the Church (early 3rd century) exclaim: 'Oh, sweet exchange! Oh, unsearchable operation!'

69 : Guilt and Curse

Galatians 1. 1–5; 3. 10–14

The purpose of Christ's death is so many-sided and far reaching that, not only do the New Testament writers give a varied presentation of it, but the same writer often interprets it differently in differing contexts. Paul is an example of this. He claims that his own apostleship is derived from God the Father who raised Christ from the dead, and so the death and resurrection of Christ are integral to the terms and authority of his apostleship (1).

Here Paul repeats what he has asserted so often that, 'Christ gave himself for our sins' (4), and on this basic principle there is no going back. But the design of the sin offering is stated in new terms. It is 'to deliver us from the present evil age' (4). This is the immediate purpose of Christ's death which makes an impact on the Christian as soon as he believes. He has to live in this age or world after his conversion, and it is an evil age that brings him under the tyranny of 'present' things. But Christ in His death 'outside the camp' (cf. Heb. 13.13) has so delivered him from this evil influence that he is emancipated from its tyranny: 'in it, but not of it' is his motto. Christ has not only delivered the Christian's soul from guilt but He has placed his strength and inspiration outside the world-order, and has fixed his goal and hope in an age that is still future.

The second passage (3.10–14) brings us deeper into what

it involved for Christ to suffer for sin. Christ found mankind under the curse involved in having broken the moral law of God (Deut. 27.26; Gal. 3.10), the central law of their own being—incapable of giving it obedience in heart and life. Such obedience was the only condition of life as long as man was answerable to the law. Christ, however, has brought a new principle of living into human experience, the principle of faith. But faith is life-giving and life-controlling only because it makes contact with Christ in His death.

This brings Paul to deal once more with what Christ has done for us in dying. He redeemed us from the curse of a law that we had broken, and that now demanded retribution. But to do this He had to accept the curse for Himself, and the fact that He actually did so was exemplified in His death on a *cross* (cf. Deut. 21.23). Because He has taken our curse, God's blessings promised to the world through Abraham, can be ours (14).

This perhaps gives us our most awesome insight into what death 'for our sins' meant for Jesus Christ as He bore them 'in his body on the tree' (cf. 1 Pet. 2.24).

70 : Far and Near

Ephesians 2. 11–22

Here Paul shows that God's purpose in the death of Christ was to bring those who were far away near to Him, and to blessing.

The far-away ones were, in this case, the Gentiles, whom the Jews regarded as aliens. Such an attitude has plenty of modern counterparts. But Jewish exclusivism apart, they were indeed without any relationship to Christ, without any fellowship with the spiritual people of God, and foreigners to all the blessings of the divine covenants made with Israel (12).

While this was their spiritual position, their spiritual condition was no better, for they had no valid hope, and were not conscious of God's presence in the world. In that condition and position the gospel of Christ reached them, and the transformation took place. In being united to Christ by faith they were, as regards position, brought into a state of nearness on the basis of Christ's sacrifice and, as regards condition, they entered into possession of the divine peace (13 f.).

In thus making Gentiles as well as Jews partakers of His peace, Christ brought them together in unity, and broke down the barrier of legalism that separated them. This unity was no mere external coming together; it removed the cause of enmity between Jew and Gentile in abolishing these legal enactments, so dear to the Jews, as no longer binding on Christ's people (15). Thus He brought the two parties together to constitute a new body, in enjoyment of peace with God and peace with one another. Christ, through His Cross killed the enmity, and gave the peace of reconciliation both to the distant Gentiles and the privileged Jews (17 f., cf. John **20**.19). He revealed Himself as the one way of access to God.

The blessings enjoyed because of this nearness to God are enumerated (18–22) as: being introduced by the Spirit into the Father's presence as one family (18); being given the fellowship of all Christians as fellow-citizens of God's Kingdom and members of His family (19); being incorporated in a spiritual temple based on the teaching of apostles and prophets; a temple that derives its unity from having Christ as its corner-stone (20).

This spiritual temple grows as each living stone is assigned its place—and note the practical emphasis—it is to be a *holy* temple, a place fit for God's presence (21 f.).

Thought : Would our neighbours (those 'far off') guess that we are 'near' God—that He lives in us?

71 : Christ a Saviour for All

1 Timothy 2.1–7; Titus 2.11–14

To Timothy Paul writes of the obligation resting on all Christians to pray for all men, and especially for their rulers (**2**.2). He justifies and reinforces this appeal by referring, first, to the declared will of God that all men might be saved by knowing in their personal experience the truths of the gospel. And since there is only one God, this disclosure of His will must be applicable to all men. Further, there is the provision that God has made for access to Himself. It is through a mediator, Jesus Christ, who, as human, has access to men, and, as divine, has access to God. He is mediator because of the ransom-price He paid to provide this access, and since there is only one mediator and one ransom-price, He must be available for all (5 f.).

In the letter to Titus (2.11–14) Paul states that 'the grace of God has appeared'—a reference to the coming of Christ into human history. This grace has brought salvation within the reach of all classes of men, spreading its spiritual enlightenment and moral culture throughout the world.

This culture of divine grace is seen in its restraint and constraint. Negatively, it teaches us to 'renounce irreligion and worldly passion', that is, to abandon a life of God-forgetfulness and worldly greed. Positively it teaches us how to act in all our relationships: personally, to live 'soberly', that is, with self-restraint; in society, to live 'uprightly', that is to be scrupulously just; and in relation to God, to live 'godly lives', that is, to be God-conscious and God-fearing.

The grace of God, then, gives training for this present life. For the life to come, it teaches us to look for the return of the One who redeemed us—who is *God Himself* (13). Even this unequivocal declaration of Christ's deity does not divert Paul from the practical interest of these verses—his great Christological statements are not designed to promote detached theological analysis. The divine Redeemer ransomed us to be those who would demonstrate their faith in character and conduct (14).

Questions and themes for study and discussion on Studies 67–71

1. How does Christ's redemption affect our entire personality, and not merely a part of it?

2. What evidence do you find in Christ's life that He was identifying Himself with sinners (cf. Matt. **9**.10 f.; **11**.19)? To what extent and for what purpose could this happen?

3. To what extent and in what way does Christ deliver us from the tyranny of things around us?

4. Since a temple is for the manifestation and worship of God, to what extent does Eph. **2**.21 f. indicate that the Church redeemed—men and women—shall be a manifestation of God through the ages?

5. What is the significance in practical terms within contemporary society, of the negative and positive demands of Tit. **2**.12 f.?

CHARACTER STUDIES

72 : The Centurion

Luke 7.1–10; Psalm 33

There is a ring of soldierly precision about the next person who moves into the story. We do not see the centurion of Capernaum, but we hear his voice, and we have his words. It is easy to see that he was a man of rare quality. This centurion had been seconded for special duty in a sphere of Herod Antipas' administration.

We shall meet four other centurions in the New Testament, and it is a notable fact that they were all men of strength and integrity. The centurions were the backbone of the Roman army, professional soldiers, and leaders among men. Palestine was a difficult province, and there seems no doubt that the officers picked for service there were specially chosen for their ability to manage potentially critical situations. Tacitus' account of an army mutiny on the Danube, not many years before this date, shows that the centurions of the legions were not all men of the stamp we meet in the New Testament. The mutineers of the historian's account complain bitterly of their centurions' brutality.

The officer who sought the aid of Jesus was a human soldier. He was fond of his slave, and attracted to the better side of Judaism. He was also a man of insight, who could see past the bitter, proud and legalistic leaders, suspicious of the new religious leader, and already excluding Him from the synagogues. He saw the Lord's worth, and came to Him with courtesy, reverence and faith. Observe, too, the centurion's exquisite tact. Knowing the tension which was rising between the Jewish leaders and Christ, he did not allow Him to enter his house, and approached Him correctly through Jewish mediators. It was for such qualities that this officer was chosen to represent the Empire in this tetrarchy. His daily habit of thought was that of a soldier, expecting unquestioning obedience, and taking discipline for granted. It was inevitable that he should see Christ in the framework of his thinking. We all do. According to our temperament—artistic, practical, philosophical—we see, interpret, and experience Christ.

Here was a Gentile, too, showing Israel the path of faith. When Luke wrote the story, twenty years after the events, the Gentiles were flooding into the Church. Luke himself was probably one of them. It pleased him to record the words of the simple soldier of the lakeside town, and the Lord's commendation.

73 : The Widow of Nain

Luke 7.11-18; 2 Kings 4.18-37

Nain, the modern Arab village of Nein, lies on the north-west slope of a hill between Gilboa and Tabor. It is two miles south-west of Endor, scene of Saul's tampering with death, and five miles south-east of Nazareth. It was twenty-five miles hard walking from Capernaum . . . We have been in this region before, because Shunem, where Elisha also gave a woman back her son, was not far away (Volume 6, Study 49).

The story of the widow of Nain is clearly one of those incidents which came to Luke's knowledge when he was wandering Palestine in quest of information, during Paul's enforced stay in Caesarea. It has no special connection with the fuller narrative. If, as some would have it, the notion was mendaciously to provide the Lord with an Elisha-like miracle, why not choose the exact place, and why a young man and not a child? Why, indeed, lie at all to no advantage?

There are marks of truth on the simple narrative. Look at it phrase by phrase, and observe how the poignant picture comes to life. It is told without art, in the simplest style, in all its bitter sadness. The widow need not have been out of her thirties. The girls of Palestine married early. She had long years of left-over life to live, and had now lost her last link with the days of her happiness. The world at large soon grows impatient with grief, and the sharing of sorrow is a rare virtue.

Luke writes with feeling, for all his simplicity. 'His heart went out to her,' says the NEB (13). He touched the bier, no doubt a long wicker stretcher, on which the body lay, as the pall-bearers took it to the burial place . . . And so the Lord of Life claimed the victim of death. Nothing more is known of the widow and her son. They no doubt returned to Nain, to whatever humble home and mundane task it was which the tragic visitation had invaded. But neither home nor occupation could ever be the same again after the hand of Christ had touched the thing of death. So it is always. Christ gives new life and feeds it back into the dead and dying world. Nain would be the better for its two new citizens, for they were indeed new people, both mother and son, who had known such benediction. In a sense, Christ still dwelt there, for He can dwell among men only as He dwells in the lives He has touched, and the hearts He has sanctified.

74 : John in Prison

Matthew 11.2–19; Luke 7.19–35

John lay in the dungeon of Machaerus, one of Herod's strongholds. In the murk, the heat, the squalor of his prison, doubt assailed him. The body's pain, shattered health, hope deferred, can bring darkness to the mind. Nor did all he heard suggest to John the Messiah of his valiant dreams. No conquering hero, no rider with the sword, was abroad in Israel, and doubt can thrive on self-made misconception.

The Lord in no way reproached the broken man. He sent him an answer, Eastern-fashion, in an object lesson, with the gentle suggestion that he should think more deeply and go on believing (Luke 7.22). Love, compassion, pity were abroad in the land. This was the God who was showing Himself in living flesh (John 1.18). In the synagogue sermon the Lord had broken the sentence of Isaiah before the grim phrase, 'the day of vengeance of our God' (Luke 4.19). John had his answer, and we are not told whether it brought enlightenment, calm and quietness to his harassed spirit.

And then, turning to the crowd around Him, Christ paid splendid tribute to John. He was no river reed, no tussock of the Jordan river-valley, bent like some pliant and yielding thing under the thrusting wind which poured down the great cleft from Galilee to Aqaba. He was not the princely aristocrat, clad softly and applauded at the palace gates by sycophantic crowds. He was the last and greatest of a stern prophetic line, and he saw, if he had eyes to see, the last fulfilment of all the long dream of Israel, the Coming of One . . .

At the same time John was to die before the consummation. He was not an apostle. He was never to see the Empty Tomb. He was never to know the gospel sent into a wider world, a conquest far more than his dreams. Therefore he lacked what the least of the Christians had and knew. He was never to be granted the last and deepest insight into God's plan for man. He would not live to see in Jesus either the wielder of fan or axe (Luke. 3.9, 17), or the fulfilment of Isa. 53. He demonstrated, none the less, that the saint can be tried by doubt, and what to do with doubt. . . .

> O Cross, that liftest up my head,
>   I dare not ask to fly from Thee;
> I lay in dust life's glory dead,
> And from the ground there blossoms red
>   Life that shall endless be.

> George Matheson.

75 : Simon the Pharisee

Luke 7.36–50

It is difficult to know why the disdainful Simon invited the Lord to dine with him. He provided none of the common courtesies; the cool water for the guest's dusty feet, the touch of scented oil on the hair, the kiss on the head which is still given in parts of the Middle East today. The woman who broke in upon the scene of discourtesy had seen with sorrow this neglect, and, after the fashion of the emotional East, remedied the lack with her own small phial of ointment, with unbound hair and tears.

A rabbi's house was not uncommonly open, and the stranger was free to haunt the courtyard outside the dining place in order to hear the words of worth which might fall from the great man's lips. The ancient world set less store by privacy than we do, but was much concerned about a reputation for wisdom. Hence the vivid scene described by Luke. Simon was prepared to patronize the new prophet, perhaps desired to examine His doctrine, but was unable to treat Him as an equal, or even as a guest should be treated.

His outlook is clear. Here was the very test he sought. Here, perhaps, with unexpected promptitude, was the answer, and the answer he had already half-formed, to any questions he might have asked about his guest. The Lord was perfectly well aware of the movement of His host's mind, and told His simple story. Simon saw the point, and replied that gratitude in human affairs is generally proportionate to the benefit received. His own view of sin was hardly adapted to see further than this, and he no doubt judged that there was very little which God might find amiss in him.

The carnal sin of the poor woman he could well understand and shudder at. Most people are prone to paint more darkly the sins of others than their own. Pride, disdain, discourtesy, self-esteem, and lofty contempt for those marked down as inferiors, are none the less sins to set in the list with the vices of the flesh. Simon had fulfilled his day's obligations to God. He had performed the necessary ablutions and formal prayers. The process brought little sanctification to one unable to see the pathos of grief over sin and passionate gratitude for God's forgiveness.

76 : The Women

Luke 8.1–3; Proverbs 31.1–31

Any observant reader of Luke's two books will note his interest in the activities of the women of the Church. It is a fair guess that, when he was collecting the material for his narrative, he met and questioned many women, including Mary herself. This brief note seems to intrude into his text without special relevance. Perhaps he derived the story of Simon and the parable of the debtors from one of the women, and was so reminded to place these facts on record.

We are given, incidentally, a glimpse into the Lord's means of sustenance. Joanna, the wife of Chuza, a manager of Herod's estates, is mentioned once more (Luke 24.10), and Susanna does not appear again, but they have honour enough in the brief words which close the small record (3). It is a fact in which women might take deep satisfaction that, although in the four Gospels there are references enough to the ministrations and loyalty of the women, there appears no single example of a woman hostile to Christ. Traitors, cynical schemers, cowards, brutes and hypocrites among men of all ages can find their predecessors, counterparts, and old examples in Judas, Pilate, Caiaphas, the creature who plaited a crown of thorns and the wretches who could sneer at the tormented figure on the cross. Women who imitate such conduct can find no types or predecessors in the pages of the Gospels. Even Pilate's wife held Him in reverence.

Mary of Magdala is not the woman of the previous chapter. The strange reference to the seven devils means that there was a mighty battle with evil for Mary's tortured soul. The phrase also shows that Christ does not let a sinner go. Again and again, as Mary stumbled, the Lord must have healed and lifted her. He returns to reclaim as often as evil returns to the attack.

And observe how, as with the Twelve, the Lord could take people as diverse in experience and background as Mary and Joanna, and make them one in Him. 'There is nothing which the Church needs more,' writes Professor Barclay, 'than to learn how to yoke in common harness the diverse temperaments and qualities of different people. If we are failing, it is our own fault, for, in Christ, it can be done—it has been done.' If one clear lesson more than another emerges from these studies, it is this precisely.

Questions and themes for study and discussion on Studies 72–76

1. Discuss the place of discipline in a society which tends to reject authority (cf. the Centurion).
2. Remembering John the Baptist's experience, how can the Christian deal with doubts?
3. Examine Scriptures which encourage God's people to show common courtesies. What outstanding Old and New Testament examples are there?
4. Consider the lives of women who came into contact with Christ. What qualities do they exhibit which Christians could well emulate?

THE WORK OF CHRIST

The Letter to the Hebrews

This unknown writer sets out to meet the needs of certain Jewish Christians who would seem to have lost something of their early enthusiasm for the Christian faith. In their experience of the 'offence of the Cross', and the fierce persecution that it entailed, they were in danger of drifting back into Judaism. To offset this the writer presents the superior excellence of Christianity. Particularly, he stresses the surpassing excellence of Jesus Christ over the leaders of the Old Testament Church, and of His sacrifice over all the sacrifices and rites of the Old Testament. In this entire Epistle we see Christ as Priest standing on the Godward side of man (2.17), presenting man to God and God to man.

77: The Better Religion

Hebrews 5.11–6.10

Professing Christians who are not showing the fruits of mature Christian character are here compared to children when they should be full-grown men, whose diet is milk instead of solid food. They were obviously cases of arrested development. Mature Christians had their 'faculties trained', their spiritual discernment so developed that they could distinguish between what is profitable and what is not (5.14).

There follows a plea for advance towards maturity, leaving behind those practices to which they were introduced as orthodox Jews—such elementary truths as those contained in 6. 1 f., which were common to both Judaism and Christianity. If professing Christians did not advance beyond these, they were in danger of lapsing into the old faith.

In this difficult passage, the writer instances cases of possible lapsing, which were probably hypothetical rather than real happenings. It is clear that all the cases mentioned there had a certain superficiality in their experience. Somehow they had stopped short of the reality, as is perhaps indicated by the words: 'enlightened', 'tasted', 'partakers'. It would seem a mere cashing in on experiences that were common among real Christians. In any case, they did not follow the light they received, or develop their experience of the grace of God (cf. The Parable of the Sower). Should these people fall away and renounce Christianity, they make an open rejection of Jesus as Messiah, as did those who had crucified Him on Calvary (6).

But Christians who follow after Christ, and show the fruits of faith in acts of obedience and love (10), are not in this perilous condition, since a righteous God maintains their relationship to Him unchanged, and in the final judgement will reward their loyalty.

78 : A Better Covenant

Hebrews 8

For the Jews Christianity must not be regarded as a new religion, but as a fulfilment of the old. Hence it is that the New Testament is a fulfilment of the Old Testament, and Christ the fulfilment of all the sacrifices and ritual and priest-hood of the old covenant. What the Hebrew Christians particularly missed was the visible presence and activity of their High Priest among them. It was the spirituality of the new religion and its priesthood that tested their faith. Christ was now their Priest and He was invisible and seemed so remote (4). Everything that Christ did for men was on a higher plane—that of spiritual reality, and not merely shadowy ritual. 'He died on earth, but the virtue and efficacy of His death proceeded from Heaven' (Calvin).

This was true of His sacrificial ministry; He offered Himself as the one all-sufficient sacrifice that fulfilled and terminated all others. It is also true of Christ's present ministry; He serves, not in an earthly temple, but in the Heavenly Sanctuary. There is also the fact that He is exercising this ministry under a new covenant, of which the old covenant revealed in the Old Testament was but a shadow. Christ referred to this at the Supper Table as 'my blood of the covenant' (Matt. 26.28). Of that covenant He Himself is the Mediator, that is, the One through whom its blessings are made available to men. The new covenant offers greater promises of blessing than did the old, and Jeremiah had a vision of them when he spoke of the 'new covenant' that God would make with His people, conferring a relationship to God that is spiritual and internal, and not merely ceremonial and external (Jer. **31**.31–34). Thus the urge to obedience comes, not from an external law, but from a law written on mind and heart, the urge of spiritual knowledge and spiritual love. This would make its power available and effective for all men, and not for Jews only.

Now that a new relationship has superseded the old, the elaborate ritualism of the Old Testament is like a worn-out garment, discarded and set aside (13). Thus the old Judaism, compared to Christianity, is only a shadow compared to the substance. For that reason it was utter folly for professing Christians to hanker after the old order.

79 : A Better Tabernacle

Hebrews 9. 1–14

The comparison and contrast between the old and the new still fill the writer's thought in this chapter. He is writing to Christian Jews who were well acquainted with the ritual of their old faith, and for whom a difficulty arose over the spirituality of the new faith. He points out that the shrine of their new faith is not an earthly tabernacle, but a heavenly one, and that marks the superiority of the power of Christ's priesthood on their behalf.

The Jewish tabernacle was equipped to convey to the worshippers how they could have access to God; precise instructions had to be obeyed before access was gained. Notwithstanding all this elaborate detail and equipment, only one man—the High Priest—was allowed to enter the divine Presence in the inner sanctuary beyond the dividing curtain. Even he was allowed to enter only on one day of the year, the Day of Atonement, and he was not permitted to enter without the blood of sacrifice (7). The restriction of this privilege to the High Priest alone clearly showed that it was an arrangement which would have to be superseded if access were to be given to everyone.

Furthermore, the real effectiveness of this ritual was strictly limited, since it did not confer on the worshipper the abiding blessings of pardon and peace. It was a shadow that pointed to a reality to come (9 f.).

When Christ obeyed, suffered and died for sinners, He revealed Himself as the true High Priest. As High Priest He entered the Holiest of All, the very Presence of God, to make an offering of Himself. But it was not through the blood of animal sacrifices that He entered; it was through His own blood. This does not mean, of course, that He took His own blood literally to Heaven. Rather, He entered God's presence because of His own sacrifice, blood, in this case as it often does, standing for the whole of Christ's work. In completing His offering once for all, as He did on Calvary, He obtained eternal redemption for sinners (12)—redemption from sin secured by the ransom price of His own sinless life and so having eternal validity.

Christ's offering, given to God as a spiritual sacrifice, is effective in a man's personal life, in a way in which the old sacrifices were not. It delivers from sin, and gives power to serve God with a life made clean and new (13 f.).

In this way the believing Jews were encouraged to let go their hold of the shadows of their ancient faith, in order to grasp and retain the reality.

80 : A Better Mediator

Hebrews 9. 15–28

The superiority of the new covenant over the old continues to be highlighted.

Because Christ acted as both Priest and Sacrifice when He did business with God for sinners at Calvary, so He now acts as the Mediator of the new covenant who dispenses His blessings to men. As Mediator He guarantees to all who deal with Him the possession of the inheritance that He secured by His voluntary death (15).

Just as a will amongst men does not operate until the testator dies, so it is true that Christ's death was necessary to release the blessings of the new covenant. This found ample confirmation in the fact that under the Old Testament system purification could not come to the priest or worshippers without the sprinkling of blood, teaching the larger truth that 'without the shedding of blood there is no forgiveness of sins'

(22). In this way the Old Testament worshippers had been prepared for the message of Calvary.

In the New Testament counterpart, however, everything is raised to a higher level, that of spiritual reality. Christ has entered, not into the 'Holy Place' of an earthly temple, but 'into heaven itself', to appear in the very presence of God for us (24). In that one offering He made an end of all sacrifices, since by the sacrifice of Himself He has actually and finally put away sin, that is, made an end of it (26).

There is to be a future appearing of Christ, 'not to deal with sin' (28), but to complete eternally the salvation of those for whom He died, by bringing them, body and soul, into God's immediate presence.

81 : A Better Sacrifice

Hebrews 10. 1–25

The writer again contrasts the shadows of the Old Testament ritual with the substantial reality of Christ's blessings to us. At best the Old Testament simply promised or foreshadowed a reality that was to come. These shadows did not actually deal with sin in itself, or with its guilt in the consciences of men. Hence the necessity for the continual repetitions of these sacrifices (3).

But Christ's offering accomplished everything to which the ancient sacrifices pointed. These other sacrifices were even temporarily effective only because God who prescribed them saw in them a reflection of the sacrifice of His Son. The Old Testament itself had indeed promised this reality in place of the shadows (5). But now 'the offering of the body of Jesus Christ once for all' (10), that is, the placing of His complete Manhood on the altar of Calvary for us, does take away sin, and through it we are 'sanctified', so that we can approach God.

As the result of that one completed offering, Christ is now exalted to the heavenly throne to await the fruits of His victory. He is *seated* there as a token that His sacrificial work is finished, and He is at God's *right hand* as a token that His work had found complete acceptance with God (12). And in God's good time He will be granted complete victory over all who oppose Him (cf. Phil. 2.9–11). There is, then, no need of any more offering for sin, since God declares that the sin with which Christ dealt is put out of memory as well as out of sight (17).

Christian believers must now make the fullest use of their new privileges. With the boldness of faith, and with full assurance, they can now enter into the very presence of God. They come by a way of access that is *new*, as distinct from that of the old sacrifices, and *living*, as distinct from the lifeless ritual of the past. Its newness and its living quality derive from the fact that it is through the broken Manhood of the Lord Jesus (i.e. the continuing effectiveness of His self-offering), and that He is now a living High Priest (21). Christians, therefore, need not remain at a distance from their Heavenly Father: their privilege is to draw near in sincerity and confidence. And what gives them access to their God gives access also to the fellowship of His people (25).

Thus the writer throughout his Epistle lifts the faith of the Hebrew Christians beyond all earthly ceremonies to a Reality in the presence of God.

Questions and themes for study and discussion on Studies 77–81

1. Discuss the possibility, say at a time of revival, of men cashing in on experiences that are not their own, resulting in a merely psychological or emotional, rather than a spiritual, conversion (cf. Heb. 6.4–7).

2. As shadows of a reality that was yet to be revealed, the Old Testament sacrifices teach us much concerning the New Testament faith. What are the limitations and values of Old Testament shadows and symbols for understanding the New?

3. Study the three appearances of Christ in Heb. 9. vs. 26, 24, 28.

4. In view of the fact that the Hebrews were brought halfway to the truth of the New Testament, what light does this throw on the peculiar difficulties of Christian mission to the Jews?

CHARACTER STUDIES

82 : The Galileans

Luke 8.4–15; Acts 17.22–34

The Parable of the Sower is the Lord's summary of His mission in Galilee. Some farmer on a stone-strewn hillside above the lake gave Him the illustration He sought, and all unknowingly entered the pages of the New Testament.

What does the story mean? The interpretation of parables is something of an art. The guiding rule is to seek for one simple purpose. The common faults are a perverse endeavour to force meaning into pictorial details, and to imagine secondary meanings. This story does not teach that the heart of man is foredoomed to receive or to reject the seed of God's planting. The parable of the sown seed is not an object lesson in theology or psychology. It is pure realism.

The first mission in Galilee was over. Perhaps it was less sweeping in its results than the disciples had expected. Possibly it was less dynamic in its impact than the mission of John. To meet their questions the Lord gave His parable. When the farmer sows his seed this is what always takes place. The paths through the fields absorb their quota. Nor can he always recognize the ground spoiled by the underlying rock, or invisibly corrupted by the hidden spores of useless and alien growth. So with the Word. Some folk harden the heart; some appear to respond but fail to follow out the implications; some who might have produced a rich and healthy crop are too busy with base or lesser pursuits; and some allow the deep good roots to strike down into heart and personality, and produce an abundant harvest.

Here, then, in an earthy little story, are the Galileans. Among the hills and along the lake, life was much as life is today. All unconsciously, like the mute earth beneath, society makes much preaching vain. The Galileans had their secure, contented members, at home in their affluent surroundings, who saw no relevance, found no challenge, in Christ. They had their wishful shallow types, their weaklings and their cowards . . . And they had among them men and women athirst for righteousness, who wanted of life, wanted of God, nothing but the best and noblest. It is common heresy, among those who read no history, to imagine that they live in a new world, full of new men and women, who neither think nor react as men and women once did. A. Housman put it:

> *The tree of man is never quiet :*
> *Then 'twas the Roman, now 'tis I.*

83 : Jesus' Family
Luke 8.19–21; Mark 3.31–35; John 7.1–9

The Lord was tempted 'in every respect . . . as we are' (Heb. 4.15). He knew, in this process, what it meant to suffer opposition in the intimate circle of His own family. Little is told us of this painful situation, and we have no idea what Mary thought. Nor is there any background of detail at all by which the events may be set in context and perspective.

The brothers and sisters of Christ are mentioned several times (Matt. 12.46; 13.55 f.; Mark 3.32; 6.3), and He Himself is called the 'first–born' (Luke 2.7). They are obviously the children of Mary. The story that they were the children of Joseph by an earlier marriage, or even cousins of the Lord, was invented by Jerome and others, who were beginning to develop the absurd hostility towards sex and marriage which is no part of Christianity, but belongs to the obscurantism of the Middle Ages.

The Lord cannot be accused of harshness in this context. Observe the brevity of detail, and the purpose for which the story was told. There are fifty-six words in the Greek text. The visitors were not necessarily dismissed nor coldly neglected. The Lord had perhaps delayed the commencement of His ministry till the age of thirty, so that Mary's other children could reach maturity and be in a position to sustain her. Consider, too, the fact that this must have been one of the stories which Mary told Luke or confirmed for him. It came from Peter to Mark, and Matthew may have been present when the incident took place. Why did three of the evangelists consider this small event important enough to record? Possibly because of the saying on the spiritual brotherhood (21), a truth which was deeply significant in the early Church.

Two other thoughts emerge. James the Lord's brother, became a leader of the Church (Gal. **1**.19; **2**.9; Acts **12**.17; **15**.13–29) and the writer of an epistle (Jas. **1**.1). Could there be stronger proof of the Resurrection? A man like James needed convincing. Secondly, consider the sad fact of stress in the home where one might least expect to find it. There is nothing more deeply or fiercely testing than hostility in the place where love and understanding should be supreme.

84 : The Tempest-Tossed

Luke 8.22–25; Mark 4.36–41

'And one man in his time plays many parts,' says Shakespeare. That is why we find ourselves confronting the same characters in varied moods and situations. In the story of the storm we see the men of Christ reacting to dire physical danger.

It was no less than that. The mighty trench, that scar of an ancient wound in the surface of the globe, which begins in the Beqaa between the Lebanon sierras and cuts south through the Jordan valley and the Galilee lake to the deep depression of the Dead Sea, and then climbs again to Aqaba, is a fearsome breeder of gales. Hot air rises from the furnace heat round the lower Jordan, and a funnelled stream is sucked in from the valley between the cool Lebanon snows. It swoops down to the Dead Sea and curves up to the Gulf of Aqaba. It is easy to see how Galilee, caught in its midmost descent, can become a turmoil of storm.

The disciples, tough boatmen and fishermen who knew the lake and its precarious moods well, were terrified, and had every reason to fear imminent death. Calmly, their Master slept through it all. It is moving to see the strong men of the lake turn naturally for aid to One who, in the brief months of their acquaintance, had won to this extent their trust and confidence. They had no evidence that He knew anything at all of seamanship. They did not know what they expected Him to do, or what they could ask of Him. Prayer is sometimes nothing more than a cry for His aid. And so it was that the storm-tossed band became a symbol for men and women in their desperation. So, too, we see deeply into the character of the distressed disciples. It is in such moments of crisis that men show with startling clarity what they think, that in which they place their trust, their true desires and apprehensions.

This is no myth, allegory or parable. It is a story vividly true to its environment. It is true, nevertheless, to life, real in the experience of the tempest-ridden in any sea of trouble. The Sankey hymn on the theme is well-known: 'Neither the wrath of the storm-tossed sea, nor demons, nor men or whatever it be . . .' There is a word in it for those Isaiah has in mind (54.11, 17): 'O afflicted one, storm-tossed, and not comforted . . . no weapon that is fashioned against you shall prosper . . .'

85 : The Maniac

Mark 5.1–10; Romans 7.15–25

If Gadara is the place by the lake which George Adam Smith thought he had identified, the steep declivity above the blue water may be pictured, the pleasant villas on the high slopes with a view up to Capernaum, the crowded waterfront and the high set amphitheatre, inevitable adjunct of all Greek towns, from which the audience could look, not only at the stage, but also at a wide prospect of lake and distant farmland.

But outside the clustered houses and public buildings there were tombs, and the geographer, while in the act of examining the place, saw a local peasant, he tells us, unearth a tombstone set up as a memorial to a soldier of the Fourteenth Legion. There on the stone was the Latin word which tangled like a living, evil thing with the thronging torments of the distracted inhabitant of the Gadara lakeside tombs.

It was a dark night when the Lord and His men came ashore, not a pleasant hour to be greeted with an ear-splitting yell from the gravestones among the rocks. The madman emerged with fragments of his bonds about his hands. He was held, he cried, by a legion of evil powers. He knew, as some victims of evil do not know, the immense strength of the force which possessed him. A legion, Rome's regimental unit, had become for him an awful symbol of himself. Perhaps he had once run madly from his village street, a

119

little shrieking boy, when a Roman patrol closed in to wreak vengeance for the local murder of some drunken legionary. Perhaps the traumatic memory of his parents dead and stabbed in the reddened dust, drove him to a consuming hate which ate up his mind.

Legion! It was like that, like the rising, falling boots in Kipling's Boer War poem, tramping, tramping day and night through his hot and ravaged brain, occupying cohorts of foul presences . . . and there among the tombs he saw the hated name again on the stones: Legion, Legion, Legion, till he screamed and tore things apart. And yet, some undamaged corner of the brain called for salvation, reached out and cried to the calm face he saw before him in the band of men who climbed out of the beached fishing boat.

'What is your name?' asked the Lord. 'There are so many of me moaned the man, that I am a whole legion of people.' The edge of that experience is known to all of us. 'Dear Lord, that loose lascivious face, that leers in my own soul,' wrote Studdart Kennedy, 'wilt Thou not smash it with Thy cross and make me free and whole?' Paul spoke of 'another law in his members, warring against the law of the mind . . .'

A legion of impulses, appetites, desires, invade and obliterate the personality—and 'some such grievous passions tear that only Christ can cast them out.' Christ did at Gadara, Christ still does.

86 : The Gadarenes

Mark 5.11–20; 8.34–38

The essential fact in this story is that a herd of swine was sacrificed to save the personality of a man. View it thus, and the charge of wanton destruction falls. A curious thought is preserved in a letter of T. E. Lawrence. He saw a little girl at play on the great green lawn before the exquisite façade of Wells Cathedral. Lawrence wondered at himself when the thought took shape in his mind that, if the choice were given, he would destroy the whole lovely building to save the child. Supreme respect for the value of the human person is a gift of Christianity to the world. Where Christianity is suppressed man becomes a brute in the eyes of tyrants, to be treated like a brute, a cog in a machine to be worn and worked for the good of the machine, a number on a list in another's selfish calculations, a punched pattern of holes in a computer card, cheap, expendable. The men of Gadara so viewed life. They begged Christ to go and leave them to their pig breeding. They had the Son of God with them. They preferred swine. John Oxenham wrote:

> *Rabbi, Begone!*
> *Thy powers bring loss to us and ours.*
> *Our ways are not as Thine—*
> *Thou lovest men—we, swine!*

The Gadarenes are still about. They are not hostile necessarily to the faith, but it must not, if they are to entertain it, interfere with life. It must not disrupt. It must occasion no discomfort. He interfered with the common, base ways of daily living, and presumed to set a higher value on the souls of men than on material possessions.

> *Christ went sadly,*
> *He had wrought for them a sign*
> *Of love and tenderness divine—*
> *They wanted swine.*

His presence healed men, but that was irrelevant if swine were lost, and the Ten Towns sold their place in history for pork.

In such a harsh environment the healed man was left. A principle is involved. If one cannot witness in the circle of one's daily life, it is idle to seek remoter service. Evangelism begins in our own Jerusalem. It is easy to imagine what difficulties the man of the tombs faced in society. The boat drew away with the banished Christ. Up the hill, in his borrowed cloak, and in his right mind, into the crowded land of the Ten Towns went the man from the tombs—the first apostle to the Gentiles.

Questions and themes for study and discussion on Studies 82–86

1. What guidelines for our conduct does our Lord's attitude to His family provide? Consider the tensions and loyalties involved in one's relationships with a non-Christian

family on the one hand and fellow Christians on the other.

2. The Christian and trouble—what part does Christ play in these experiences?

3. What is the significance of Christ's sending back the demoniac to his own people?

4. How should a Christian deal with opposition at home, his place of work, etc.?

5. Christ left the Gadarenes as requested. In the light of the rest of the New Testament does this say anything specific about evangelism? What should be our attitude when faced with the hostility of Communism, Islam, etc.?

THE WORK OF CHRIST

The Teaching of John

The Epistles of John and the Book of Revelation have this distinctive quality in common, that they always relate the death of Christ to sin and to its removal from the believer's life. In other words, John now is giving an ethical application of the truth, whereas in his Gospel he was giving an historical statement.

87: God is Light

1 John 1.5–2.2

When John proclaims that God is light, he is proclaiming the holiness of God's nature and the purity of His character. To walk in the light is to live in obedience to the will of God, and so develop in holiness of character. This walking in obedience has two results: it brings us into fellowship with God and with His people; and it so exposes sin that we turn to the blood of Christ for cleansing (7). The efficacy of the blood or sacrifice of Christ is seen in viewing it as an ever-flowing stream that *goes on* cleansing from sin. And it deals effectively with sin in its guilt and its power. To deny the existence of sin—as some teachers in John's day were doing—is to practise self-deception (8), while to confess it to God is to receive the two blessings of forgiveness and cleansing. For God to forgive, and not to cleanse, would be a mockery of our need. But God's character ensures against this (9).

Full and free forgiveness is not licence to sin, and God never gives permission to sin to any one. But when sin over-comes us, we do not despair, for we have an Advocate in Heaven who will act on our behalf. The word 'Advocate' in Greek really means 'one called to our side to help', and this Jesus Christ is for us. He is righteous and acts righteously on our behalf, for He Himself has fulfilled all the conditions needed for our forgiveness. He has given us authority to use

His name, for He is still our 'expiation' or 'propitiation' (AV, [KJV]) in the sight of God, the One who continues to bear the punishment our sin deserves, and the displeasure that it invokes. There is nothing exclusive about Christ's reconciliation; it is available to the whole world (2.2).

Here then is laid bare the significance of Christ's sacrifice in our personal lives. It exposes sin. But when sin is confessed, it pardons and cleanses. It is a notable fact that the greatest saints were, as Luther says, penitents all their days, confessing sin and receiving cleansing. Note that forgiveness can never belittle sin: the cost of forgiveness ensures against that.

88 : God is Love

1 John 4.7–21

Though the truth of God's love is interwoven with the entire revelation of the Old Testament, it required the coming of Jesus Christ and His death to give adequate expression to it. This disposes, once and for all, of the misconception that Christ died to make God love us. On the contrary, it was the love of God that sent His Son into the world 'that we might live through him' (9). Love, in its very nature, seeks expression, just as a spring seeks an outlet, and God's love found such expression that we can say: 'In this is love' (10). The fact that it was when we were unlovely and unlovable that God gave this supreme manifestation of His love to us constitutes the surpassing wonder of the gospel. But it was holy love that could not deal with sin unless 'expiation' or 'propitiation' (AV, [KJV]) was made, and love designed and made that offering. This is a manifestation, not only of the immensity, but also of the sanctity of divine love.

This love of God is the source of all true love in us, and so our inspiration to love one another (19). When one hand is laid on the altar of divine love, the other is laid on the heart of a brother, so that we become to him the conductors of the love of God.

To this love in its supreme manifestation we bear witness as Christians, for we proclaim that God sent His Son as 'the Saviour of the world' (14). This is the first time that this term occurs (but cf. John 4.42), and it opens up limitless possibilities in the realm of final salvation. It envisages a great future for the world in the way of final restoration and healing from the ravages of sin. We believe that before the world will have run its course, Christ will prove and justify this title given to Him—the Saviour of the world—in the final reality of a saved world. Even though much will be lost (for impenitence is a sober reality), it is but as the barren and blighted branches of the tree cast off; the tree itself will be saved.

We who bear His name must share Christ's attitude to the whole world in hating its sin and seeking its salvation, confident that it is not to be abandoned to sin and the devil. Ours is a vista of glorious and confident hope. Contrast this with the stark pessimism of Robert Burns:

> I backward cast my e'e on prospects drear,
> And forward tho' I cannot see, I guess and fear.

89 : Christ the Overcomer

1 John 5.4–9; John 19.31–37

In our last study Christ was presented by John as the Saviour of the world. Here He is presented as the Overcomer of the world. In the first case it is the world of human beings, in the second it is the world of moral evil. The argument is that, as Christ in His death and resurrection showed Himself victor over the forces of evil, so those who are linked to Him by faith share His victory. This victory is defined in terms of faith, and faith is defined as believing that Jesus is the Son of God (4 f.). If we believe that Jesus Christ is, in very truth, the Son of God, then the world, and all it stands for finds its rightful place.

John now seems to take up two historical facts in the life of Christ—His baptism in the Jordan and His death on the cross—and asserts that, because of this, Christ came 'by water and blood' (6). In His baptism He began His life-work by identifying Himself with those He came to save, and in His death He completed that work of identification and reconciliation. Bearing in mind John's use in his Gospel of the combination 'blood and water' (19.31–37), we may accept that he has in mind here also the twofold efficacy of

Christ's work in atoning and cleansing, one or the other of which had been disputed by certain teachers of John's day. It is undoubtedly true that, to the atoning and cleansing virtue of Christ's death, the Spirit has witnessed and is witnessing.

John in his Gospel (**19**.31–37) makes use of two phenomena that were present in Christ's death—that His bones were not broken and that His body was pierced—as fulfilment of two Old Testament prophecies, Exod. **12**.46 and Zech. **12**.10, respectively. The first identifies Christ with the Passover Lamb, the other with the Suffering Servant. Its spiritual significance may be that Christ's death did not break or disrupt the Church which is His body, but that it became the power that leads men to repentance and gathers them into the Church.

The saying of James Denney needs pondering: 'Christianity is as real as the blood of Christ' (*The Death of Christ*, p. 154).

90 : The Lamb as Revealer

Revelation 5

The book or scroll that John saw, bearing seven seals, was probably of the nature of a will or last testament. Apparently it contained truth relating to the future that was not yet known to men. John 'wept much' at the thought that this testament was not to be known or put into operation (4). But he was assured that 'the Lion of the tribe of Judah, the Root of David' had conquered and, because of His victory, had acquired the right to read, and the power to execute, its contents (5).

What John saw, however, was not a lion, but a little lamb (the word is a diminutive in Greek), bearing the appearance of sacrifice, yet standing alive in the centre of the throne, having all the tokens of complete power (seven horns) and of perfect wisdom (seven eyes). It is noteworthy that when the Lamb took hold of the scroll to break its seal and unfold its message, there was a chorus of assent and adoration from the heavenly host. This was taken up by the whole universe, adding its adoration to the Lamb (12 f.).

It is clear that Christ is represented under both figures,

126

Lion and Lamb. In John's vision, however, the Lion recedes, and the Lamb fills the picture completely. It was under this figure that John had what was probably his first recognition of the Messiahship of Jesus of Nazareth (John 1.35–37), and his vision is still, significantly, the same.

There is also the fact that, though the Lamb was alive and active (standing in the centre of the throne), He still had the signs of death about Him ('as though it had been slain'). It is clear, therefore, that it was because of His redeeming sacrifice that the Lamb was entrusted to reveal and to execute the will of God. This programme is still being carried out through the gospel of the Cross.

Let James Denney interpret the scene: 'It is really a pictorial way of saying that redeeming love is the last reality in the universe, which all praise must exalt and to which everything else must be subordinate' (*The Death of Christ,* p. 136).

91 : The Lamb as Shepherd

Revelation 7.9–17

It is significant that in the closing scenes of the Book of Revelation the Lamb still shares the Throne with God Almighty, 'throned face to face in equal deity' (Milton).

The redeemed of humanity, seen now triumphant in heaven, stand before the Throne of God and of the Lamb, bearing the symbols of purity (white robes), and of victory (palm branches). With shouts of praise they attribute their salvation to 'God and the Lamb', or as we would say, to God through Jesus Christ their Saviour (10).

The white-robed throng are identified as those who have come out of 'the great tribulation' (14). It is not necessary to ascribe this designation to any special period of church history; it seems better to accept it as relating to a general condition common to all who witness and suffer for their Saviour. Their robes, however, were washed, not in the tribulation, but in the efficacy of the Lamb's sacrifice, through which every vestige of sin had at last been removed.

The dominating factor in the scene, however, is that the One who sits on the Throne shall radiate His Presence throughout: (lit: 'make His shekinah to rest on them', a reference to the light in the Holy of Holies of the ancient Temple). The privations of the journey are past, and replaced by perfect rest in perfect surroundings.

It is noteworthy that the Lamb is still the Shepherd, He will care for them throughout eternity, satisfying heart and mind completely (17). Heaven's rest is not stagnation (15). It is perfection, but a perfection which somehow will develop with all hindrances removed. However little we can understand it, it, at least, spells unimpeded progress for the spiritual nature of the redeemed.

Questions and themes for study and discussion on Studies 87–91

1. Note the three false views in relation to sin hinted at here, and their modern counterparts:
   (1) Sin is of no consequence (1 John 1.6), cf. some schools of psychology.
   (2) We are not responsible for our sin (1 John 1.8), cf. Some aspects of evolutionary thought.
   (3) Sin does not exist (1 John 1.10), cf. Christian Science.

2. In what respect do you think there is *eternal* significance in the death of Christ?

3. To what extent may John's vision of the Lamb indicate that our first acquaintance with Christ as personal Saviour interprets our vision of Him for ever (cf. John 1.29–36)?

4. If there is moral perfection in Heaven, and yet unimpeded progress, in what directions may we develop?